"A CLEAR AND PRACTICAL GUIDE TO LIFTING
WILTED SPIRITS."

—*Ms* Magazine

Even the most successful and healthy among us can benefit
from resolving unfinished business. Whether you are
facing a personal crisis, a sudden change, or the desire to
get out of a rut, A FRESH START can help you move
through the unresolved issues of your past and grasp your
new future. Dr. Leonard Felder has the answers for people
who are asking questions about how to change:

—What does it take to break out of a rut?
—How do you let go of the past?
—How do you repair strained relations with difficult family
  members?
—How do you keep other people from dumping their
  baggage on you?

"Helpful, informative and fun to read. You'll enjoy yourself
while learning."

—Dr. Irene Kassorla, author of *Nice Girls Do*

(For more acclaim, please turn page . . .)

LEONARD FELDER, Ph.D., a psychologist and syndicated
columnist, is co-author of four books, including the
acclaimed bestseller, *Making Peace With Your Parents*,
which won the 1985 Book of the Year Award from
Medical Self-Care Magazine. A frequent lecturer, keynote
speaker, and talk-show guest, he also writes articles for
several major magazines. Dr. Felder received the 1987
Distinguished Merit Citation of the National Conference of
Christians and Jews for his volunteer work to combat
racism, sexism, and religious prejudice. He lives in Santa
Monica, California.

A FRESH START

How to Let Go of Emotional Baggage and Enjoy Your Life Again

Leonard Felder, Ph.D.

A SIGNET BOOK

NEW AMERICAN LIBRARY

A DIVISION OF PENGUIN BOOKS USA INC.

PUBLISHER'S NOTE

The ideas, procedures and suggestions contained in this book are not intended as a substitute for consulting with your physician. All matters regarding your health require medical supervision.

Copyright © 1987 by Leonard Felder

A *Fresh Start* previously appeared in an NAL Books hardcover edition published by New American Library, a division of Penguin Books USA Inc., and simultaneously in Canada by The New American library of Canada Limited (now Penguin Books Canada Limited).

ACKNOWLEDGMENTS

Grateful acknowledgment is made to Paul Simon Music, Inc., for permission to reprint the lyric from "Slip Slidin' Away" by Paul Simon, copyright © 1977.

for Linda Schorin,
my partner, teacher, wife, and friend

Contents

Acknowledgments

I have been fortunate to meet and work with several mentors who shared their gifts for psychology and writing. I offer my thanks and gratitude to M. Robert Syme, James Michael, Rowland Shepard, Sean Austin, Tom Bonoma, David Bayer, Blair Brown Hoyt, Sonny Stokes, Sondra Ray, Binnie Dansby, Wendy Piuck, Adelaide Bry, Harold Bloomfield and Sirah Vettese Bloomfield, Charlotte Mayerson, Linda Seger, and Lew Richfield.

This book is based on the experiences and insights of many individuals who spoke with me as friends, relatives, clients, and colleagues. I would like to thank all those who contributed to the development of this project, especially Lucky Altman, Andrea Bayer, Mary Ellen Bayer, Francine Browner, Catherine Coulson, Teri Davis, Angela and Jeff Dondanville, Glen Effertz, Mel Eisman, Ted Falcon, Frank and Kathy Fochetta, Melinda Garcia, Evone Lespier, Arlene Levin, Jim Levin, Bret Lyon, Catherine Mahlin, Alice March, Chris Miller, Victor Moreno, Glen Poling, Peter Reiss, Janice and Craig Ruff, Barbara Schlain, Karen Schweibish, Robin Siegal, Paul Silver, Susan Steinmetz, Janet Sternfeld, Neil Van Steenbergen, Linda Waddington, David and Doretta Winkelman.

Special thanks are given to those who added their creative talents, friendship, and professionalism to this book, including my literary agents Maureen and Eric Lasher, my editor Michaela Hamilton, and my lecture agent Nancy Nelson.

I would like to offer my love, appreciation, and thanks to my parents, Martin and Ena Felder, to all my family members, and especially to Helen Rothenberg Felder.

Finally, I want to thank Linda Schorin for her creative suggestions, her honesty, and her love. I am very lucky to have such a strong and courageous partner.

Author's Note

To protect confidentiality, the names and identifying details in the case histories reported within this book have been changed.

Anyone with a history of psychiatric disorder, who feels emotionally unstable, or is taking major tranquilizers or antidepressant medication should not do the exercises in this book without first consulting a qualified mental health professional.

Introduction

A few years ago, a woman named Patricia told me about the following experience:

> Last Saturday night on my birthday,
> a few close friends arranged a
> small party. I had to go of course,
> but if you want to know the truth
> I didn't feel much like celebrating.
>
> I always thought by the time I reached
> this age, I would have cleared up
> certain issues. Yet here I am,
> not growing any younger, and still
> unsure of why my life isn't turning out
> the way I hoped it would.
>
> While driving to the party, I had
> this awful thought. I imagined myself
> losing control of the car and swerving
> across the center divider. It scared me.
> I've never had an image like that before.

If you met Patricia in person, you'd never suspect she was depressed, or that her birthday had raised some difficult issues. Like many people, Patricia looks as though she has everything under control even when she's hurting inside. Fortunately, she had the good sense to talk to someone about the thoughts and images that were running through her mind.

1

I remember my first impression of her the day she approached me at a lecture I was giving. Intelligent and energetic, she looked like the kind of creative woman who might be running her own business and enjoying a satisfying personal life. Yet when she talked about herself, she revealed some painful concerns:

> I never thought I'd be this age and
> still be without someone to love.
> Or that I'd still be stuck in a job
> that feels so unlike who I am.
>
> I've often told myself, "Don't worry,
> Pat, there's plenty of time." But now
> I'm beginning to wonder if I'll ever
> get my life together the way I wish it
> could be.

Like many of us, Patricia is asking important questions and not settling for easy answers. If you know you are capable of so much more, and yet something has been holding you back, it's time to begin asking why.

When Patricia first came to see me for advice, she was afraid her moods and questions meant there was something "wrong" with her. As I told her then, "Wanting to improve certain parts of your life is nothing to be ashamed about. Each of us has unresolved issues that need a closer look. It doesn't mean you're neurotic or that something is 'wrong' with you. It simply means you have the courage not to settle for less than what your life might be."

Over the next two years, Patricia began using the techniques that are described in the chapters of this book. She began with inner work—discovering the reasons why she had been unable to build a satisfying long-term relationship. She also unraveled what was holding her back from starting her own business and began to resolve the self-doubts that she had developed as a result of her upbringing.

Gradually, Patricia found ways to use these insights in her daily life. She met someone with whom she began to establish an outstanding relationship. She started to make some changes in her work life and in the way she dealt with people.

What began as a feeling of depression and frustration slowly became the start of a new phase of Patricia's life. As she described recently:

> The biggest change is that I'm finally in a good relationship and I've developed a job that feels like me. But there's also a more subtle change my friends have noticed. For years I would talk about making changes and then not follow through. Now I've broken that habit—if I say I'm going to work on something to make it better, I don't give up so easily.

Are You Ready to Make Some Improvements?

This book is about making a fresh start in the most crucial areas of your life. It provides a step-by-step method for seeking answers to the difficult questions we ask ourselves from time to time. With case studies and exercises, it is an exploration of how people turn the bad things that happen to them into opportunities for growth and recovery.

Like Patricia, many of us have felt blocked at times from making the improvements in our lives we deeply desire. We say we're ready to let go of a bad habit, yet it sticks like glue. We talk about fixing a dissatisfying situation, but it doesn't seem to get better. Or we try to recover from a loss or setback, only to find leftover feelings still hold us back from taking the next step forward.

If you or a close friend or loved one has been talking about making changes that never seem to happen, this book will help you unravel the reasons why. If you have found it painfully difficult to get moving again after falling into a rut, you might be glad to know there are powerful exercises you can use to work through the barriers that stand between you and a healthier direction.

A Personal Note

When I began to write this book, I realized much of the material came not only from my work as a psychologist but also from experiences in my personal life. Several times in the past, I have found myself up against difficult situations I was not prepared for. I wish at those times someone had handed me a book like this to help me understand what I was going through and what some creative options might be.

I was fourteen years old and quite unprepared to deal with the complex emotions when my mother died of cancer. The pain of losing her didn't end at the funeral as some people at the time told me it would. Weeks and months later, the tears flowed and the empty feeling within me remained just as strong.

Watching a loved one suffer from a terrible illness and seeing her die is not something that goes away quickly. I wish someone had given me the kind of advice and support that will be discussed in this book: that recovering from a painful experience requires time and patience; that there are stages you need to go through to heal the hurt you feel inside; and that these stages of recovery allow you to feel whole again and appreciate your life and loved ones even more than before.

During those nights of lying awake with tears in my eyes and unanswered questions, I had no idea how long the feelings of sadness would last. Nor did I understand how to begin the slow process of making a new beginning. If you or someone you know is going through a similar struggle at the present time, this book can offer support and assistance. Even if the loss you suffered took place a long time ago, you might still benefit from healing the leftover hurt that hasn't gone away on its own.

Several years later I went through another rough period. This time it wasn't a person dying but a dream of mine that was shattered. After years of education and anticipation, my first choice of career turned out to be a mistake. In my heart I knew I wanted to be a psychologist and writer. To be "practical" I had chosen instead to become "a three-piece suit" and work for a large corporation.

Every day at work, I spent a lot of time wishing that I was anywhere but stuck doing projects that felt meaningless and going to meetings that dragged on much longer than necessary. To keep up appearances, I smiled and pretended to be enthusiastic about my work. Yet inside I felt like screaming. Where was the life of meaning and purpose I dreamed about in high school and college? Where was the sense of satisfaction that my work was of value or that my efforts were making a difference?

The advice I received at the time was not to make waves. "You can't expect too much from one's work," I was told. If only someone had talked about creative ways to make a smooth transition onto a more satisfying career path. Instead it took years before I found the courage to break out of my rut. It took many years beyond that before I found a way to balance the need to pay the bills with the needs to do something meaningful and fulfilling. This book talks about the steps and stages that are required to find a way to express your unique gifts in the world. I won't tell you the road is easy, but I will offer techniques and true stories of how others created a second chance in their search for a life of meaning.

Finally, there was another period of my life when I could have used a book like this. The breakup of my first marriage left a deep hurt inside me that wouldn't go away. My ex-wife and I both shared such high hopes for our relationship and still were unable to overcome the difficulties that confronted us.

I remember wondering then if I'd ever feel safe again to trust someone so deeply. I felt as though I had failed at probably the most important commitment in my life up to that time. What I needed during those moments was a sense that these are common feelings—that others before me have gone through similar hard times and come out with renewed strength.

Fortunately, I found supportive friends and counselors who could help me work through the issues raised by my divorce. Recovery took time and patience, but it did finally happen. The disappointment from my first marriage taught me a great deal and has helped make my second marriage stronger. Once again, I discovered that inner healing is possible and can lead to a fresh start that provides tremendous happiness.

How to Get the Most from This Book

Regardless of your age or circumstances, it's never too late to begin resolving the issues that have the power to hold you back from your goals and keep you awake at night. In the chapters of this book, you will learn what it takes to break out of a painful rut, no matter how long you've been stuck there. You will also be shown creative ways to overcome the resistances that come up whenever you or I attempt to make changes in our lives.

As a psychologist, there is nothing more exciting than those times when someone I counsel makes a satisfying recovery from a bad situation. I can't guarantee that every new beginning you attempt as a result of this book will be easy or successful. But I can offer you my support and the best advice I know how to give.

Many people buy self-help books, put them on the shelf without reading them, and then resent that the book didn't help. Others read the books from cover to cover, but don't use any of the techniques in their own lives. They too wind up feeling discouraged that the book talked about changes and yet nothing happened for them personally.

On the other hand, some women and men not only read but apply the insights and exercises to their daily lives. They are the ones who truly benefit. Please use this book not only as a story of how others have made changes in their lives, but as a tool for action in your own life. It is meant to give you options you might not have considered and to provide support as you take on the challenges of your life.

I wish you the very best,

Leonard Felder

Leonard Felder, Ph.D.

What Does It Take to Break Out of a Rut?

1

> Slip sliding away, slip sliding away.
> You know the nearer your destination
> the more you're slip sliding away.
> —Paul Simon

If you take a glass jar with air holes at the top and you put some flies inside the jar, the flies will buzz around frantically trying to get out of the cramped container. However, if you keep the ventilated jar closed a long time, something fascinating happens.

If the perforated lid has been on long enough, when you finally take it off the flies don't escape. That's right— even though the lid is off and the opening is clear, the flies that are so used to circling in the cramped jar will continue to do so. Just when they get close to the opening, they go right back to flying the same patterns that keep them imprisoned.

Unfortunately, human beings have the same problem. We often carry so much emotional baggage from long ago that our lives feel like a burden and we fall into painful ruts. Rather than learning and growing from our frustrating setbacks, we have this strange habit of reenacting similar traumas over and over again.

A fundamental insight of psychology is that whatever is unresolved from the past will find a way to keep disrupting your present and future. The best way to make a positive new beginning is to uncover what unfinished business from long ago is keeping you stuck.

Breaking Free

This is a book about making changes and improvements in your life. It's about breaking free of a painful rut and finding a way to bring your goals to fruition.

For example, think about your own situation for a moment. What are the new beginnings you would like this book to help you start working toward? Give an honest answer to each of the following questions. Remember, it doesn't cost you anything to dream a little.

—If you could improve one thing about your primary love relationship (or the lack of one), what would it be?

—If you could change one thing about your work life or your daily activities at home, what would you change?

—If you could clear up one lingering problem with a certain member of your family, what would that entail?

—If you could heal any unresolved hurt from your past, what would you like to heal or resolve?

We all have parts of our lives that could use some improvement. Yet if you want to make real progress in any of these areas, there's something crucial you need to know: There are two opposing methods you can use when you seek to make changes in the difficult areas of your life. Which method you pick could make the difference between satisfaction and the frustration of "slip sliding away" just when you get close to reaching your desired destination.

Here are the two choices you can make whenever you seek to change or improve some part of your life:

The "Asking for Trouble Method"

This is the choice most people make, and it causes a great deal of heartache and disappointment. The "Asking for Trouble Method" is when you try to fix some area of your life while failing to resolve the emotional baggage you carry inside about that issue. Sooner or later the unresolved questions come back to haunt you.

For example, here is an illustration of what happens when we try to deny or ignore our unfinished business from the past. See if this sounds like you or someone you know.

The Crowded Bedroom

You've been hurt by love before, but instead of resolving the issues from past relationships, you have decided to fall in love again. Only this time you are convinced your new partner is "nothing like your ex."

Now imagine it's late at night and the two of you are feeling romantic. Then suddenly your loved one does or says something that reminds your subconscious of something painful from the past. It could be that your current partner is criticizing you the way a former lover or family member once criticized you. Or your current partner isn't listening to your feelings and needs, much like an ex-partner or parent used to ignore what you asked for.

Suddenly you are flooded with emotions of hurt and anger. You try to keep them inside but they spill out on your current partner, even though these feelings have more to do with someone from long ago.

You have tried for years to ignore your unfinished business about love, but now the bedroom seems overcrowded with painful memories. You no longer feel romantic at all, because your current partner has made the mistake of unintentionally opening the lock on your emotional baggage from the past.

In the "Asking for Trouble Method," you would never stop to ask yourself, "What issue from the past is causing me to feel so upset right now?" Instead, you would do what most couples do—argue, accuse and try to get back at each other because of reawakened hurts from long ago.

None of us wants to keep having the same arguments and setbacks over and over again. Yet when you choose the "Asking for Trouble Method" and pretend you don't have any emotional baggage to deal with, that's what you get. As the philosopher George Santayana wrote, "Those who cannot remember the past are condemned to repeat it." Especially in your most important relationships, ignoring your unspoken hurts from the past is the reason why they keep reappearing in a slightly different form with every partner you love.

The "Letting Go Method"

This is the alternative choice, the one most people rarely make but the one that can be more successful and satisfying. In the "Letting Go Method," the trick is to remember that *whenever you are upset with someone in the present moment, you can safely assume it is because they have retriggered an unresolved hurt from your past.* It's time to stop blaming and attacking the person in front of you. Instead you will make much better progress if you look within and ask yourself, "What issue from the past is causing me to feel so upset right now?"

The "Letting Go Method" can dramatically improve the way you deal with painful situations and difficult people. Instead of feeling victimized whenever things turn out badly, you are given a second chance—an opportunity to find out what can be learned from this situation and what can be improved.

Here are some illustrations of why the "Letting Go Method" is so powerful and effective in a variety of settings:

> When you and someone you love are having an argument, you can either become enemies and accuse each other of every bad feeling that's raging inside you . . .
> *Or*, you can stop, unwind, and find out what each of you brings to the situation from past hurts and bad experiences. Then, as allies instead of bitter adversaries, you can work together to find a resolution that is satisfying to both partners.

> When you and someone you work with are having a disagreement, you can either outshout each other until one side gives up and says, "I'm tired of dealing with this stubborn mule" . . .
> *Or*, you can stop and find out what each of you brings to the situation from past experiences and hard-earned wisdom. It's amazing what can happen when two people stop arguing long enough to unravel why they feel the way they do. Instead of misreading each other, you finally discover what makes both of you tick.

> When you and someone in your family get on each other's nerves, you can either wallow in your frustration . . .
> *Or*, you can stop and sort out what incidents from long ago have made the two of you so impatient and judgmental with one another. Only when you get to the bottom of why you are so intolerant of each other can you begin building a healthier way of relating.

In the "Letting Go Method," your arguments are shorter and your enjoyment of life is much greater. Instead of remaining oblivious to the reasons why things aren't turning out right, this method allows you to unravel the crucial feelings and issues that need to be resolved.

Here's an illustration of how the "Letting Go Method"

can restore your enjoyment and help you make improvements in a difficult area of your life.

The Couple Everyone Was Rooting For

A long time before Janet and Robert came to me for advice, they were friends of mine. I knew Robert many years ago when he was married to his first wife, Ellen, who died suddenly at a very young age. Robert was left to raise two small children. I met Janet a few years later when she and Robert were first beginning to talk about getting married.

Some weddings bring a tear to the corner of your eye; others cause you to use one or two tissues to wipe the tears. At Robert and Janet's ceremony, even those who usually don't cry in public agreed it was "a four-Kleenex affair." Most of Robert's friends and relatives were crying because they knew how much Robert suffered when his first wife Ellen died. Most of Janet's guests were crying because they saw how happy Janet was to have found a handsome and caring man like Robert after the battles she endured with her first husband.

Robert and Janet are a couple everyone was rooting for. So nearly everyone was shocked when only two years after the wedding, they began talking about getting a divorce.

The problem in Robert and Janet's marriage was the same issue that affects millions of other couples—they were taking out on each other the unresolved hurts each of them carried from prior experiences. Yet like most couples, they were quick to deny that the past had anything to do with their current troubles.

Even though Robert insisted he would never compare Janet to his first wife Ellen, whose death he tried not to think about, Janet saw the situation differently. According to her, "Robert and his two children always seem to expect me to do things exactly the way Ellen did. It's hard to compete with a saint. I'm sure Ellen had her flaws, but Robert and his children can't seem to remember a single imperfection." Like many widows and widowers, Robert was struggling at love because of unfinished business from the previous loss he suffered.

On the other side of the conflict, there were Janet's unresolved issues from long ago. Although Janet insisted that she had no leftover baggage from her previous marriage, Robert felt differently. According to him, "After Janet's been on the phone with her ex fighting about weekend visits or late checks, all I have to do is look the wrong way and I become the bad guy. I can't count the number of times her anger at him got dumped on me." Like many who have felt mistreated by a previous love, Janet wanted to be open to a new relationship but carried a number of resistances from her prior battles.

Like the rest of us, Janet and Robert held high expectations that they had found someone to love. Yet in each of our lives, if we continue to walk into every romantic situation with an armload of overfilled baggage from previous hurts and disappointments, it's nearly impossible to make the current relationship successful.

Before coming in for counseling, Robert and Janet were enmeshed in the "Asking for Trouble Method" of accusing each other and denying their own unresolved issues from the past. One of the great ironies of life is that we often take out on innocent loved ones the unfinished business we have with not-so-innocent people from long ago. Many parents unload their frustrations on their children because they haven't been able to resolve their hurts from their own childhoods. Many lovers and spouses unload their frustrations on each other because they haven't been able to work through their painful unexpressed hurts from other relationships.

When I talked to Janet and Robert about the importance of getting to the root of why they were arguing so much, they were still a little hesitant. "Why do we have to look at the past when so much has changed since then," Janet asked. It made me think of Santayana's quote again, "Those who cannot remember the past are condemned to repeat it."

Only when their fights got worse did Janet and Robert begin to realize their relationship wasn't going to survive several more rounds of accusations and denials. As Robert commented, "Our marriage has so much potential and yet we're at each other's throats so often. Maybe it's time we tried something new." Finally, they were ready to stop asking for trouble and start letting go of the past.

The first step was for Robert and Janet to begin unraveling the unresolved issues that they each had brought separately into the relationship. For Robert, that meant finally looking into the ways his first wife's death was affecting his second marriage.

After years of denying that he had anything but love and admiration for his deceased wife Ellen, Robert began to explore the feelings of anger and abandonment he had never been able to discuss prior to our sessions. With tears running down his cheeks, Robert finally began to work through the complex emotions he had locked inside from losing a loved one. He also began to discuss openly the problems that existed in his first marriage, which he had never been willing to discuss since Ellen's death. Only after letting go of many unspoken hurts about his first marriage was Robert able to start recognizing the unrealistic expectations and criticisms he had put on his second wife Janet.

In Janet's case, the inner work she needed to do was primarily about the ways in which she had kept silent when she felt mistreated by her ex-husband. Instead of letting those resentments fester inside and then burst out at Robert, Janet began to resolve the leftover anger and mistrust that were carried over from her first marriage.

After both partners began making progress in understanding the obstacles that came from previous relationships, they were ready to start improving the ways they related to each other. Over a period of several months, Janet and Robert began to explore healthier ways of communicating their needs and concerns to one another. They also began to look at problem-solving in the relationship as something they could do as allies rather than adversaries.

Instead of getting divorced or continuing to mistreat each other, Robert and Janet discovered what most people find out when they use the "Letting Go Method." They realized that the key to solving current problems is to unravel how they are created by unresolved issues from long ago. With a renewed sense of commitment to working through their problems, Robert and Janet saved their relationship from a breakup and began the slow process of building a satisfying, long-lasting marriage. As Robert described recently, "For a while there, I began to look at Janet as my enemy, the person I had to defeat in order to feel victorious. Now I'm beginning to see her as my partner, my lifelong partner in working through our issues from the past and building a satisfying future."

A Powerful New Skill

What are the unresolved hurts you carry into each new love relationship? What are the nagging fears and self-doubts you bring to each new work situation? What are the hidden resentments you take along to every family phone call or get-together? You can pretend these unresolved feelings don't exist, or you can begin the liberating process of working through your unfinished business.

The remainder of this book will explore the terrible costs we pay when we fall back into the habit of ignoring or denying our hurts from the past. It will also help you develop a powerful new skill—the ability to sort out your inner feelings whenever you find that a new beginning is being thwarted by issues from long ago.

Learning to let go of emotional baggage is not a skill that is taught in school or in our families. Yet it might be the most useful and rewarding tool you develop in your lifetime. Clearly none of us wants to continue to be held back by the unfortunate things that have happened to us in the past. As you read the chapters that follow, be aware that you are engaging in an important process of self-discovery and growth. Instead of remaining a victim of your past, you will be gaining insights and strength because of what you have been through.

How Do You Let Go of the Past?

2

> We should be careful to get out of an experience
> only the wisdom that is in it—and stop there;
> lest we be like the cat that sits on a hot stove lid.
> She will never sit down on a hot stove lid again—
> and that is well; but also she will never sit down
> on a cold one anymore.
>
> —Mark Twain

Working through the emotional baggage that holds you back in crucial areas of your life is *not* a passive activity. You can't simply wish for a change or wait for time to heal all wounds. It might be easier if you could, but the problem remains that every hurt from the past has a way of lodging in your memory. From that day forward you may subconsciously react with fear or anger whenever you encounter a similar person or situation.

For example, years after someone makes a cruel remark about the way you look, you may find yourself still overreacting whenever someone comments on your appearance. A loved one says, "You look nice tonight," and you doubt this person is telling you the truth. Or someone makes a tiny suggestion about your clothes, your hair, or your shape and you feel enraged. Or you find yourself extremely anxious about your appearance before an important meeting or social event. You may not be aware of the exact memories, but it's helpful to begin unraveling where those debilitating feelings come from.

Many people are reluctant to clean up unfinished business or deal with hurts from long ago. They argue that "what's done is done . . . I don't look back."

Clearly, none of us wants to stir up pain from ancient history, yet none of us wants to keep letting those same memories interfere with the progress we want to make in our love life, work life, and family relationships.

The "Four Levels of Letting Go," which I am about to describe and illustrate, do *not* require excessive or unnecessary wallowing in times gone by. You can get to the heart of a current obstacle without suffering a lot of pain and discomfort if you understand and carefully follow these techniques. Cleaning out your system need not be a painful burden. In fact, if done correctly it can be a tremendously rewarding experience.

Learning to use these techniques in your daily life will help you regain your momentum every time a fresh start or step forward is threatened by the reemergence of emotional baggage from the past. Having these tools at your disposal will give you valuable insights and restored peace of mind during those moments when you get sidetracked from important goals. Instead of feeling defeated whenever issues from the past disrupt your life, these techniques will enable you to uncover the internal obstacle so you can successfully get on with your plans.

The Four Levels of Letting Go

In the next several pages, I will explain a technique for working through emotional baggage and making a fresh start in the important areas of your life. Rather than just reading the descriptions, take a few moments to do the exercises. Only by applying these techniques to a current problem in your life will you discover their usefulness. These guidelines and exercises have been successful for women and men from a variety of backgrounds. They could be helpful to you if you follow the instructions carefully.

The First Level of Letting Go: AWARENESS

Think about an issue, decision, or memory that has been on your mind lately. Or think about a disagreement or conflict you've been having with someone at home, at work, or in your family. For example, here are several possible situations you can use in this exercise. Stop for a moment and select the one you would like to understand and resolve most. Choose one of the following:

—A conflict you are having with your current partner or an ex.
—A relationship decision you have been reluctant to make.
—An unhealthy pattern you want to eliminate from your love life.

—A conflict you are having at work or had in a previous job.
—A career decision you have been struggling with.
—An unhealthy work situation or habit pattern you want to change.

—A conflict you are having with a parent, child, sibling, or in-law.
—Guilt feelings you have about a situation in your family.
—An unhealthy pattern you've acquired for relating to a member of your family.

Before reading further, you are to choose *one* incident or situation from the above list that currently weighs on your mind.

What is the issue or conflict you would like to work on?

Now comes the opportunity to gain a new perspective on the situation. One of the great ironies of human emotions is that we are never upset only for the reason we think. Every time we are angry, sad, or filled with uncertainties it has something to do with the current situation but, more importantly, it has a lot to do with some unfinished business from the past.

Looking deeper at the issue or conflict you chose above, what does this situation resemble from your past experiences, emotional hurts or habitual patterns? Letting your thoughts wander freely through your memory banks, what does the issue or conflict you chose for this exercise bring to mind?

To uncover the past incident or series of experiences that resemble the current upset, you may need to ask yourself some thought-provoking questions. For instance, when in the past have you felt a similar bind or conflict that might provide a clue about the situation you are working to resolve in this exercise? What in your childhood resembles the predicament or emotions you are experiencing now?

Take your time looking for a connection between the present conflict and a past memory. Then, when you have an idea, describe the past event that comes to mind.

The current issue reminds you of what from the past?

Sometimes the past hurt that underlies the current upset doesn't come to mind right away. You may need to set aside a few minutes of quiet, uninterrupted time to let your thoughts wander to incidents from the past that are similar to your current decision or conflict. In some instances, you may need to discuss the question of "What does this current issue remind me of from the past?" with a friend, counselor, or support group of people who have shared a similar experience.

The more you practice this technique of stopping, relaxing, and looking for a connection between current upsets and prior emotional hurts, the quicker you can resolve painful emotions and the less often you will dump your anger or frustration on others. Eventually you will become adept at recognizing the presence of emotional baggage as soon as a current incident arouses feelings from long ago. Instead of feeling victimized or confused, you will quickly be able to understand what unresolved emotional hurts were touched off. Rather than blowing up at someone you care about or sulking silently, you will be able to communicate what you are upset about, what issues from the past need resolution, and what the other person can do to be of assistance.

For example, Lisa and Peter recently got married and, like many couples, they soon found themselves having an argument about money. Peter accused Lisa of outspending her portion of their monthly budget. Lisa accused Peter of being dictatorial with his sermons about saving money. In no time at all, they were both feeling angry and distant from each other.

To break the vicious cycle of accusations and hurt feelings, Lisa and Peter decided to use the Awareness Technique described above. They stopped arguing long enough to look within at what kinds of emotional baggage each was bringing to the situation.

When Lisa asked herself, "What does this conflict remind me of?," she wasn't exactly sure. But she had a vague sense that it was a familiar feeling to have someone lording it over her on the subject of money. So she asked the question in a different way, "Who did a similar power trip on me in the past?" Immediately she knew the answer. The way Peter was treating her about money was a lot like the way her father bossed her around whenever she needed a few extra dollars. It also brought back memories of her ex-husband acting superior because he was the major breadwinner (and yet he broke several financial agreements with Lisa).

Instead of assuming all her anger had to do with Peter and the immediate situation, Lisa became aware that a good portion of her anger had to do with leftover issues with these two other men, her father and her ex-husband, who both made Peter seem like an angel by comparison.

When Peter asked himself, "What does this conflict remind me of?," nothing came to mind at first. After asking the question several times in different ways, he still couldn't find a connection to the past. Then I asked him a very direct question many people find helpful. I asked, "While growing up in your family, was there ever a similar conflict between your parents? Did they ever argue about money in a similar way?"

Being asked to describe his parents' relationship brought back a flood of memories for Peter. When he was a teenager, his parents fought a great deal about money and later split up in a bitterly contested divorce. Peter realized he was resembling his father when he attempted to belittle and control Lisa on the subject of keeping budgets.

Since he didn't want to repeat his father's abusive style, Peter knew he had to do something to change his own behavior. Unless he became more constructive and less authoritarian about financial matters, he was in jeopardy of ruining their relationship.

Please note: While some psychoanalysts might insist that it takes several years of three-times-a-week therapy to uncover painful memories from long ago, many other counselors and therapists have experienced quicker insights simply by asking clients questions like those I've mentioned.

When using this Awareness Technique on your own, don't try to dig to the deepest levels of your subconscious. In most cases, that isn't necessary. What the Four

Levels of Letting Go allow you to do is achieve a break-through by uncovering a less-mysterious connection between past hurts and present dilemmas.

If asking yourself the first question—"What does this current issue remind me of from the past?"—draws a blank, then you need to ask a different, more creative question such as, "When in the past did someone treat me this way?" or, "When did I go through a conflict similar to the one I'm facing now?"

Even if the Awareness you achieve is merely a top layer of a deeper mystery, it can still be beneficial. For example, Peter and Lisa may have only uncovered a surface layer of insight about their money and power struggles. Yet in their case it was sufficient to help them stop mistreating each other and start improving their relationship.

As partners rather than adversaries, Peter and Lisa soon were able to work through their money issues without letting unresolved feelings from the past turn their discussions into a bitter struggle for control. Their case illustrates what happens when you interrupt an argument with a loved one, co-worker or family member to ask yourself, "What does this conflict remind me of?" By becoming aware of the past experiences that underlie your strong emotions, you can more easily resolve the current situation. By unraveling the past, you gain new insights into ways to address your current dilemmas.

The Second Level of Letting Go: HIDDEN BELIEFS

Now we come to one of the most intriguing parts of working through emotional baggage. We will be uncovering hidden beliefs and important life decisions we made based on painful incidents that happened long ago.

Focusing again on the current issue or disagreement you chose earlier to work on in this exercise:

What is the issue or conflict you are seeking to resolve?

Now remembering what you came up with in the First Level of Letting Go, keep in mind:

This current issue reminded you of what from the past?

Once you have this past incident in mind, consider what decisions you might have made at that time to protect yourself from additional hurts. Be creative and insightful as you imagine *what beliefs about yourself, other people, or similar situations you might have formed as a protective reaction to what happened to you. What fears or habits did you take on because of this incident?*

For example, each of us has been rejected or disappointed by a loved one or close family member we thought we could trust. As a result of the pain we felt, we may have taken on a variety of subtle beliefs that now give us trouble in relationships. What makes you nervous or "not yourself" when you are with someone you love? What makes you test someone or not trust a loved one even when he or she is being trustworthy? What makes you question whether someone really loves you when they act in a certain way?

If you are like most people who have loved and lost, you probably took on damaging beliefs about yourself, such as the fear that you aren't lovable enough, attractive enough, interesting enough, or successful enough. Or you might have taken on harmful beliefs about other people, such as the fear that anyone you trust will take advantage of you, or that anyone who says he or she loves you must not be all that terrific if they've "settled" for someone like you. Even if these beliefs are buried deep in your subconscious, they can still have a devastating impact on your ability to relax, be yourself, and survive the ups and downs of a loving relationship.

The subtle beliefs we carry inside as a result of previous hurts are at times irrational or overgeneralized. Yet they still affect our current decisions and moods because

our minds are trying to protect us from getting hurt
again. You can say you want to let go of a self-defeating
pattern that you have outgrown, but unless you come to
terms with the underlying beliefs that resulted from a
long ago incident your efforts will be futile.

Here is a powerful way to uncover a hidden belief that
may be holding you back from your potential in an
important area of your life:

Bringing to mind once again the issue you are working
on in this exercise (the one you looked into on the
previous pages), ask yourself a few questions to uncover
the hidden beliefs associated with this problem area.

—What might you have decided long ago was the best
way to prevent future hurts of a similar nature?

—What did you think you had to give up or stop doing
in order to protect yourself?

—What did you believe you had to become or do in
order to feel safe again or win back what you felt you
had lost?

—What did you fear other people or similar situations
would be like as a result of what you experienced?

Based on these incidents from long ago, what hidden
beliefs do you have about yourself, other people, or
similar situations?

*What self-limiting decision did you make at that time
which has been affecting your life ever since?*

Now begins the process of unraveling the belief so that
you will eventually be freed of its harmful and limiting
effects. Looking at the fears or attitudes you uncovered
above, ask yourself the following two questions:

In what ways are these beliefs still accurate or useful?
In what ways do they still protect you or give you
accurate early warnings that trouble might be brewing?

Think about a time when this belief or decision helped you avoid or get out of a dangerous situation.

In what ways are these beliefs no longer appropriate or even harmful to you today? In what ways are you like the cat that not only won't sit on a hot stove lid again, but also won't sit on a cold one anymore?

Think about a time when this belief or decision held you back in some important area of your life.

Once again, you may want to discuss these questions with a friend, counselor, or support group. Unraveling the hidden beliefs brought on by a painful incident from the past often requires patience and a conscious search that can be aided by others who have worked through similar traumas in their own lives. None of us wanted to take on the fears, insecurities, or self-defeating patterns that life's difficulties have saddled us with. Yet now you have reached a crossroads. You can let your hidden beliefs continue to undermine your best intentions or you can begin the rewarding process of working through even the most stubborn habits.

The Worrier

Danielle's case is one illustration of how this Second Level of Letting Go can gradually change a long-term pattern that is holding you back. Like many thoughtful people who have had a difficult life, Danielle is a worrier. Even when things are going well in her relationships or her work, she worries that it's all going to fall apart. For years Danielle has taken courses in positive thinking and self-esteem without any noticeable change in her habit of worrying too much and enjoying life too little.

Recently, Danielle used the steps listed above to ask herself what started her as a worrier. What incident or series of events in the past gave her the belief system that worrying was the way to go? How did someone with so much potential become so overly cautious and anxious whenever she took a risk in her love life or her career?

At first Danielle couldn't pinpoint one traumatic event that explained her habit of chronically worrying. *Quite often it is not a single incident but a series of events that causes us to take on harmful fears and limiting beliefs.* You may need to look back to a period in your life when several things changed abruptly to alter the way you viewed yourself or the world around you. Or it could be a time when your sense of comfort or safety was dramatically upset.

In Danielle's case, that period of upheaval occurred around the time she was twelve years old. During that year, Danielle remembered changing from a relatively optimistic young woman into a cautious and worrisome person as a result of several losses she suffered within a short period of time. Her grandmother, who lived with the family, died suddenly of a heart attack. Danielle's father lost his job, and the family had to move to another city, far from Danielle's two closest girlfriends. In addition, the second month they were in the new city, Danielle lost her other closest companion, a lovable golden retriever, who was run over by a car in front of their home. In less than a year, Danielle had lost several important sources of support and stability. In the mind of a young person, that can feel like the end of the world.

Danielle remembers becoming extremely quiet and cut off from her new classmates and from her family during that time. She admits, "I didn't have anyone I could talk to, so I turned inward. I must have made a decision, without knowing it or saying it to anyone, that I wasn't going to let painful things like that happen to me again. And the only way I knew how to prevent that kind of pain from repeating itself was by becoming overly cautious and doing everything possible to keep things in order."

Even though it had been many years since Danielle suffered these losses, the fears and habits she took on as a result were still affecting her life in crucial ways. When I asked Danielle to make a list of the hidden beliefs that could have resulted from the upheavals of her thirteenth year, she wrote out the following:

> I must have decided that I had to hold on tightly to anyone I cared about because I feared I might lose them. That's made me extremely possessive and clutchy with my romantic partners. I hold on so tightly the other person has to get away from me in order to breathe.

> I definitely became more cautious, mulling over decisions longer than necessary. That's been a handicap in my work life as I've failed to trust my instincts or assert my ideas for fear of being incorrect.

> I clearly started believing that change was always going to be painful and that the more I avoided taking risks the less I might suffer. That has caused me to stay in relationships and stay at jobs that I knew weren't working. There's a long delay between when I know instinctively it's time for a change and when I allow myself to take the next step forward.

> I began second-guessing myself and wondering if I hadn't done something awful to bring about all the things that went wrong. That's been a problem several times in my life when I've felt guilty for bad things that I couldn't possibly have caused. There's still a fear inside me that says I'm being punished again, just like I once thought I was being punished when those things happened to me at the age of twelve.

Once Danielle had gotten to the heart of why she had become a worrier, the next challenge became how to catch herself each time she began to worry excessively or act in an overly cautious or controlling manner. Breaking her habit of expecting the worst wasn't easy, yet over a period of months Danielle began to make noticeable progress. Whenever she noticed her thoughts turning dark and worrisome, she made sure she talked to a friend or wrote in her journal. Sorting out her realistic fears from her unrealistic worrying, Danielle gradually learned how to take risks and trust her instincts better in both her love life and her career. Instead of seeing her challenges through the frightened eyes of a worrier, she eventually began to enjoy a much greater level of confidence and competence in her life.

Like Danielle, we each have fears and self-defeating habits that stem from long-ago incidents we haven't fully resolved. Instead of remaining unaware of what is at the root of a current upset or disappointment, using these techniques can prevent minor conflicts from turning into major crises. When you notice yourself worrying or becoming anxious over a difficult challenge, stop and ask yourself what memories from the past this issue resembles. Then go deeper to find out what hidden beliefs, fears and obstacles you may have acquired from the previous bad experience. Only then will you know how to avoid repeating the same mistakes over and over again. Only then will you have regained your freedom and not be run by painful emotions from long ago.

The Third Level of Letting Go: RELEASING

Unresolved baggage from the past not only clutters up our minds but also lodges itself in parts of our bodies. Unless we physically release the leftover remnants of hurts from long ago we are left with a variety of physical tensions, aches, and pains we don't deserve.

For example, have you ever noticed that many people who feel burdened by past experiences tend to walk in a hunched fashion and actually look like they have a weight on their shoulders? Those of us who feel held back by past disappointments often internalize these emotions with respiratory and stomach problems. Many people who carry unresolved issues from the past or delay making decisions about the future suffer from sleeping problems and tension headaches. It's nearly impossible to be fully productive or healthy when you are bogged down by issues from the past.

On the other hand, when you use any one of several methods to physically release leftover emotions from long ago, life stops feeling like such a burden. Muscle tensions and physical blockages have a chance to relax and unwind. Your body feels lighter and healthier after using these techniques. Your mind is once again freer and your spirit and enthusiasm feel restored.

The question is not whether you have pain and anger stored inside from past hurts; part of being alive means there are resentments to work through. Rather, the challenge is finding a safe and appropriate way to let go of the leftover emotions without hurting yourself or anyone else. When anger is channeled and released safely, you not only avoid taking it out on someone else but also gain an energizing burst of creativity.

The suggestions which follow have been used by people from all walks of life to safely release pent-up feelings. Executives, homemakers, clergy, accountants, athletes, artists—no one is immune from the need to let go of rage in a way that won't cause any harm to ourselves and those we love. I urge you not to just read these instructions but to begin using these techniques whenever you feel bottled up with emotions, especially when you are overreacting to a current incident because of residual rage from long ago. (Please note that several

of these exercises are not new. You may have heard
people suggest them in the past. However, what would
be *new* is if you and I used these powerful releasers more
often to get unresolved hurts out of our system.)

Focusing again on the issue you chose to resolve earlier,
picture the individual or situation clearly in mind. Then
use one or more of the following suggestions to physically get any leftover pain out of your system:

—*The Angry Letter.* Write an angry letter (at least one
page and no more than twenty) to the person who
hurt you, describing such things as: "I resent . . . ,"
"I want you to know . . . ," "I will no longer tolerate . . . ," "I will no longer keep silent when . . . ,"
and "I regret . . ." *UNDER NO CIRCUMSTANCES
WILL YOU SEND THIS LETTER OR LET THE
OTHER PERSON KNOW OF ITS EXISTENCE.*
The purpose of physically writing out your anger is
to get it out of your system in a safe manner. After
you have released the rage you feel inside, you will
be better able to take the next *constructive* step
forward.

—*The Artist's Release.* Draw, paint, or mold clay into a
visual representation of the angry feelings and hurt-
ful incident you have kept inside. Let the colors,
shapes, strokes, and images express and release your
emotions. Use this exercise to let go of pent-up feelings, and do *not* show the drawing, painting, or
sculpture to the person in question.

—*The Scream.* Close your eyes and imagine the sound
of your own scream. This technique is done silently;
you do not need to strain your voice screaming.
Rather, by imagining the sound of your own scream
filling up your mind, the room around you, and the
entire city, you will achieve a healthy release that
can be done in complete privacy. Do this several
times until you feel a breakthrough.

—*The Fantasy.* Close your eyes and imagine a scene in your mind's eye in which you have complete freedom to ventilate your resentments and regrets to the other person while the other person does nothing but listen without interrupting, and apologize without defending. Even if this could not happen in real life (or if the person is unavailable, uncooperative, or no longer living), experiencing it in your imagination can have the same emotional impact on your psyche. If you have trouble imagining the other person, do this exercise by talking to a photograph of him or her. Spend at least ten minutes describing your feelings toward this person and then imagine several apologies and positive acknowledgments being given to you in a supportive fashion.

—*The Shake-Out.* Either with or without music, spend ten to twenty minutes shaking out the anger, tension, and resentment that has been bottled inside you about this situation. Let yourself make faces, wiggle your arms and legs, and imagine yourself releasing pounds of emotional baggage with each physical gesture. I call this shake-out "Spazzercize" and the more uninhibited you let yourself be, the better. The only caution is to make sure you don't injure yourself with any jarring motions.

—*The Fist.* Work out physically what you cannot express in words. Pound a mattress, a bolster pillow, or a firm seat cushion for at least ten minutes with this person or situation in mind. Pound a hunk of clay or an imaginary punching bag with this unfinished business in your thoughts. Please note that the purpose of this exercise is to release your anger *safely*. Any activity that hurts another person or yourself is not necessary or effective.

—*The Journal Dialogue.* Imagine that the other person or the conflict situation is a reflection of some disowned part of yourself, some aspect you have been ignoring or suppressing that has something to tell you now. Write a dialogue in your journal or on sheets of paper in which "you yourself" and "you the other person" take turns ventilating feelings and releasing unresolved issues. Find out what each side is doing from its own point of view. When both sides have had a complete opportunity to express all the resentments, regrets and strategies they feel strongly about, continue the dialogue until both sides have asked for and received clarification of each other's needs. Only when you fully understand and appreciate both points of view are you ready to complete the dialogue by suggesting a resolution both sides can accept.

—*Get Support.* If you feel blocked or unable to complete at least one of the above options, give yourself a short rest before trying again. Sometimes it takes several attempts before the pent-up feelings are released. You may want to talk with a friend, counselor, or support group who can listen to your feelings without interrupting or making judgments. The importance of finding a safe and harmless way to get these leftover feelings from painful emotional hurts out of your system cannot be overstated. Achieving a return to full emotional and physical well-being may depend on your persistence in finding a safe release for the stored-up anger or sadness that has been festering inside.

This level of letting go provides many people with their strongest breakthroughs, yet at the same time it is the one part of the exercise that many people avoid. We human beings are terrified of admitting we have anger stored inside. We are afraid of letting it out. Many people would, in the words of Woody Allen, "rather grow a tumor" than express strong emotions from a recent or ancient conflict.

Even if you are having trouble finding a way to physically release your leftover anger from a past incident, don't give up. Many people have used creativity and persistence to achieve vitally important breakthroughs after years of feeling stuck. Here are a few examples to give you some ideas:

• A woman I counseled whose name is Barbara had a host of unresolved feelings and pent-up anger for a man she had dated in college who had forced her to have sex against her will. According to a recent study, 25 percent of women in college today have encountered examples of "date rape" or "acquaintance rape" from men they thought they could trust.*

Like many who have been physically violated in this way, Barbara kept her rage locked inside and was afraid to risk letting it out. She began writing an angry letter but stopped after a few sentences. Then she attempted to imagine herself telling off the man who had forced himself on her, but again she stopped. She feared even an imaginary confrontation with this individual was too threatening.

When I suggested she work through some of her suppressed rage by imagining the ten strongest women she knew backing her up in the imaginary confrontation, she could do it successfully. Finally Barbara let the feelings of shock and disgust come pouring out. Even though it had been several years since the incident and Barbara was releasing her anger only in a visualized scenario, she experienced a tremendous release and reempowerment.

• When a seminar participant named Steven wanted to find a way to release his pent-up anger toward a former boss who had fired him unjustly, he first tried to draw his

*See *Ms*. magazine, October 1985, pages 56–59.

emotions. Yet Steven found himself repeatedly drawing his former boss as a towering giant who could not be confronted.

Then Steven tried a different approach—pounding a mattress until he felt his anger filling his chest with energy. No longer feeling small and helpless, Steven sat down and wrote an uninhibited letter (which he agreed not to send) to this former employer. In the letter, Steven got beyond his normally polite and soft-spoken demeanor as he spewed out his emotions at being mistreated and fired. By the time he had written several pages, Steven described, "I felt ten pounds lighter and a lot more confident that this was not going to happen again."

• When Bonnie attempted to work through her emotional baggage about her younger brother, who died in a car accident at the age of twenty, she felt blocked. Like many people seeking a new beginning after the death of a loved one for whom they have both positive and negative memories, Bonnie felt guilty for possessing mixed emotions. She describes how "I had enough trouble getting angry with my brother when he was alive. Now that he's no longer living I feel terrible even thinking angry thoughts about him or the fact he left with so much unresolved between us."

I advised Bonnie to sit down with a photograph of her brother and talk to the photo as though it were him. The only way she could restore her love for her brother and fully get on with her life was by releasing the anger and sadness that was sapping her energy. After twenty minutes of describing her resentments and regrets to her brother's photograph, Bonnie was finally able to tell him the loving things his death had never allowed her to share. Rather than being a morbid or painful experience, releasing pent-up feelings toward someone who is no longer living (a parent, child, friend, spouse, lover, relative, or adversary) allows us finally to feel resolved about his or her death. The best way to honor someone's memory is not to deny your mixed feelings but to work through your unresolved issues in a safe and effective way.

Please note that you need to be gentle with yourself when doing these releasing techniques. If tears begin to flow make sure you take the time to breathe, relax, and not interrupt the sadness that needs to be released. If anger comes up, be careful not to misdirect it toward innocent bystanders or loved ones. You may want to take a swim, a walk, a relaxing bath, or a short rest before attempting to return to normal activities. If you continue to feel anxious or upset from the issues you are releasing, be sure to get support from someone who can listen to you without interrupting or judging. The more support you give yourself and get from others, the easier it will be to let go of the past and proceed forward.

The Fourth Level of Letting Go:
MAKING A FRESH START

Finally we come to the best part of working through hurts from the past—it's time to take the next step forward in a part of your life that has been held back. Whether the issue is your love life, family situation, career, or another personal challenge, now is the chance to reap the benefits of your inner work. This is the opportunity for you to test whether or not you've let go of the past sufficiently to get on with your life.

Going back to Chapter One for a moment, what were the fresh starts you envisioned for yourself? What were the steps forward you wanted to make in several important areas of your life?

Looking back to the problem area you chose to work on in the current chapter, what might be a constructive improvement for that situation? What next step of progress are you now ready to take on after having worked through your unresolved feelings about this issue?

Before you attempt to make any fresh start, however, there's something important you need to understand. Too often people take a workshop, read a book, or do an exercise and then immediately assume everything has changed—that all their problems should magically disappear. Or they expect unrealistic goals to come true simply because their adrenaline and optimism tell them anything is possible.

I don't want you to set yourself up for disappointment. The fresh starts and steps forward you pursue as a result of what you read in this book need to be realistic. The last thing I want you to do is ruin the good work you've done in the first three levels of letting go. That can happen to anyone if you make bad assumptions or foolish choices about what your next step should be.

For example, I once worked with a woman who did a terrific job letting go of unresolved feelings from a bad marriage she had finally gotten out of her system. Yet when it came time to choose her next step forward, she was unrealistic. Her goal was that her next relationship should have absolutely no resemblance and none of the same problems as her previous marriage. She wanted her inner work to have a magical result—that she would never again encounter any of the same traits or conflicts she resented in her ex-husband.

When I heard her goal, my first reaction was that she might be setting herself up for disappointment. Her desire to find a problem-free relationship with no past resemblances meant she'd probably be disappointed with any human being she got involved with. As I suggested to her, it's safe to assume that all future relationships will show at least some similarities to past relationships. Many of the same problems will reappear as future tests of how much progress you've made.

However, the difference is how well you deal with your feelings and communicate your needs next time. The fresh start to aim for is not that all problems will magically disappear, but that having worked through your emotional baggage you will be more creative and effective in resolving these problems when they arise again. The issues that drove you crazy or caused a breakup in a previous romantic partnership don't disappear from your life forever. Rather, they become the test issues you need to watch for, handle carefully, and resolve with good communication in your current or future romance. Making a fresh start doesn't mean living in a fantasy world with no conflicts—it means doing a much better job trusting your instincts and negotiating for your needs the next time similar conflicts arise.

Another example of a fresh start that is bound to fail is illustrated by an artist I counseled who had suffered several business setbacks. This creative artist/businessman had done a great job working through his emotional baggage about partners who had betrayed him, assistants who had let him down, and mistakes of his own from which he'd finally learned. Yet when I asked him what his next step forward was going to be, he answered, "I'm going to make sure the next time I start a business, I won't have to rely on anyone. From now on, the only person I'll rely on is myself."

Clearly this person was setting an unrealistic goal. As long as he wanted to be in business, have relationships or remain a member of the human race, he would need to deal with other people. The fresh starts he needed to pursue were how to choose partners and assistants more effectively, how to do business more skillfully, and not how to bury his head in the sand or try to sell his artwork from an isolated mountaintop.

The important factor in any new beginning is to realize what lessons and new inner strengths you can take from the previous experience and bring to the next challenge. The progress you make in your love life or your work life is not that everything becomes a breeze. Rather, it is that you learn to be more skillful at resolving conflicts before they reach the crisis point and that you take better care of yourself in difficult situations.

Bearing in mind that your goals should be realistic and that even a small step forward constitutes progress, what is a fresh start your inner work in this chapter has prepared you to take? What is the next step forward you want to attempt in your love life, work life, family situation, or other personal challenges? What is the next small improvement you will make happen in this area of your life for which you have been resolving issues from the past?

Stop for a moment and picture in your mind's eye what this new beginning will look like, feel like and be like.

As you think about what your next challenge should be, remember not to push yourself in a direction you are not ready to go just yet. If you are still recovering from a painful loss or disappointment, don't attempt to jump into a highly stressful and difficult situation right away. Take a less drastic step forward and build on one small success at a time.

When people set goals that are unrealistic or too ambitious, they aren't really making a solid start at all. Instead they are setting themselves up for a "quick fizzle," a new beginning that starts out with a lot of adrenaline and optimism only to dissolve into failure and dissatisfaction. When you take your next step forward in the areas of your life you are seeking to improve, keep in mind the differences between a quick fizzle and a solid start.

A quick fizzle:

—Rushes into the next challenge without really working through your emotional baggage from previous challenges.

—Sets unrealistic goals that assume everything is going to be different and wonderful next time.

—Is ready to give up the minute a familiar hurt from long ago shows up again.

—Thinks you must be doing something wrong if the new situation isn't perfect or easy.

—Doesn't recognize that even after you've learned certain lessons there are still more lessons to learn.

—Doesn't give you room to make mistakes or mid-course adjustments.

—Promises more than you can deliver.

—Makes you feel like a failure for not living up to unrealistic pictures that your life is supposed to be easier than it actually is.

On the other hand, these are the characteristics to keep in mind if you intend to make a solid start that has a good chance of leading to satisfaction.

A solid start:

—Recognizes that emotional baggage from the past may show up at any time and needs to be resolved.

—Takes small steps forward and appreciates the hard work that goes into any minuscule changes or improvements.

—Accepts that mistakes are bound to happen and realizes that every setback has a lesson contained in it.

—Has a long-range goal in mind but focuses more on the practical details of making each small success happen.

—Is willing to change tactics to get around obstacles while keeping the overall direction in mind.

—Doesn't rush into bad risks, but strengthens your persistence and creativity for pursuing good risks.

—Knows how to ask others for assistance and emotional support, so that you don't have to feel you're doing it all alone.

What most people tend to forget when they are taking on new challenges is how difficult it is to let go of old habits, even if we intellectually know those old habits are self-defeating. You have to remember your emotional memory will always be whispering to you that it's not safe to move forward in your love life, work life or family situation. Even if you know it's time to take the next constructive step, a small frightened voice inside may be saying, "Wait! Don't! Not yet!"

My advice is to be supportive and loving to that frightened voice inside yourself without letting it keep you from moving forward. The struggle to grow as a human being while at the same time fearing the next step reminds me of a wonderful story that is told at Passover, the Jewish holiday that celebrates the escape from slavery in Egypt to the freedom that was so unfamiliar and frightening to a people who had spent so long living under the domination of others.

According to the tradition, when Moses first talked about leading the Jews out of Egypt, they all wanted to go. Slavery under the pharaohs was terrible and Moses' description of freedom sounded glorious. But then things got rough. The Egyptians were in hot pursuit, the arid desert and the formidable Red Sea loomed as insurmountable obstacles for those who wanted to be free. Many thought about turning back. Very few believed they would make it across the Red Sea and the desert to reach freedom in their promised land.

From a psychological point of view, this story of holding back just at the edge of freedom is a powerful metaphor of what goes on in our own lives. If you or I were in the desert with almost no water and the Egyptian soldiers closing in, would we have stepped into the Red Sea and hoped we didn't drown? Surely, the enslavement we had known for years was awful, but at the same time it was familiar, predictable, orderly. On the other hand, freedom was an unknown—risky, unfamiliar, no guarantees, it might not last. Needless to say, arguments broke out and many wanted to turn back. Most people are more comfortable holding onto their emotional enslavements than risking something new and uncertain.

When you or I set out to make a fresh start, we are leaving behind the familiar, the predictable, the orderly. We are traveling into a sea of emotions that will at times feel unfamiliar, unpredictable, and chaotic. There are no guarantees that your fresh starts will turn out as planned. The Red Sea does what it does and we can only keep moving forward in the right direction.

Don't put yourself down for having fears, for wanting to turn back, for sometimes falling short of your potential. But whatever you do, don't turn back! Even if it takes longer or requires more effort than you anticipated, your freedom from the limitations of your past is worth it. Your journey to a better emotional state will justify the fears and obstacles you have to cross.

What to Expect
in the Remainder of the Book

In the remaining chapters, you will see how to apply these "Four Levels of Letting Go" to specific areas of your life. Each chapter will focus on a different challenge: relationships, work, family, spirituality, overcoming procrastination, dealing with critical people. Within each of these discussions you will see how others have used these exercises and techniques to make significant improvements in areas of their life that were stuck or dissatisfying.

Even though you might be tempted at this point to put the book aside and take on the next challenge we have been discussing, I recommend you go further and read the chapters first. You will pick up additional clues as to how you can improve your situation. You will discover several obstacles and mistakes that others have made and which can be avoided if you recognize them early enough. You will also gain added support and motivation for making your fresh starts come to fruition.

Each of us has known the disappointment of thinking we are moving forward in our lives only to find we are repeating the same habits. In the chapters that follow, you will be shown several ways to break out of ruts that have affected your life for too long. Only by getting to the heart of what is holding you back will you finally be able to improve the most crucial parts of your life.

What Stands Between You and the Kind of Relationship You Want?

3

> Well, what is a relationship? It's about two people having tremendous weaknesses and vulnerabilities, like we all do, and one person being able to strengthen the other in their areas of vulnerability. And vice versa.
> You need each other. You bolster each other. You complete each other, passion and romance aside.
>
> —Jane Fonda

A few weeks after her husband Jonathan died following a long illness, a friend of mine named Tracy was rummaging through drawers in their study when she came across Jonathan's private journal. Her first reaction was not to read it because, when Jonathan was alive, he and Tracy promised each other not to look at their private diaries.

The next day, however, Tracy couldn't get the journal out of her mind. Cautiously opening it, she began to read several entries and eventually came across something that surprised her. Jonathan had written page after page of things he was unhappy about concerning their marriage—habits he wanted to change, issues he had never brought up.

The more Tracy read the dissatisfactions Jonathan had

never expressed about their relationship, the more her eyes filled with tears.

"Why didn't we ever take the time to discuss these things?" she asked herself. "What were we afraid of that we kept so much unspoken?"

One of the great tragedies in life is when two people who love and need each other can't talk to each other. It not only happens to couples who separate and divorce but also afflicts those who stay together year after year.

Whether you've been with someone three weeks, three years, or thirty-three years, every intimate relationship has issues that cry out for resolution and plenty of room for improvement. In most cases, however, we keep our needs silent and wait until it's too late before taking seriously the tensions between us. Or we stuff our resentments inside for too long until one day we lash out angrily at the person we once adored. Even the strongest love between two people can't survive if we are afraid to work through the conflicts between us.

Why is it so hard to communicate in an intimate relationship? Why do we have so much trouble articulating essential information such as: "This is what I enjoy and what I don't enjoy when we make love"; "This is what I need from you when I'm upset or stressed"; "This is how we might divide our responsibilities around the house"; and "This is what I'd like to clear up so we can be closer."

Why do we think about making a fresh start, either by improving the current relationship or finding a new one with greater potential, yet hold back and do nothing? Why do we have so much clarity and so many good ideas about our friends' relationships and so much unspoken about our own?

An important reason why loved ones have trouble talking to each other is because none of us acts the same in an intimate relationship as we do in other areas of our lives. Someone who is decisive in business might be terrified of decisions such as making a commitment, moving in together, sharing finances, getting married, or having children. Someone who is relaxed and confident with most challenges can be anxious and insecure in love. Someone who is creative and spontaneous with old friends can be the most rigid and unimaginative person when he or she is with a spouse.

When two people fall in love, move in together, or get married, it tends to bring out parts of their personalities they barely knew existed. For example, there are two extremes many people fall into when they are in a relationship—"The Pleaser" and "The Demander." Most of us have a little of both. As you read the following descriptions of these two patterns, notice how much they apply to you and your current or former partner.

"The Pleaser"

Terrified of being rejected, the pleaser will do just about anything to make his or her partner happy. The problem is most pleasers are unable to express their *own* needs in a relationship. If you ask them, "Is everything all right?," they'll say "Everything's fine" even if they are upset or dissatisfied. If you ask them, "What do you want?," they'll sound like a parrot and reply, "What do *you* want?"

Here are some familiar habits that keep pleasers from being able to express their needs or take care of the things they are dissatisfied with in a relationship. See how many of these ring true for you:

> I never come right out and say what I need because I don't want my partner to think I'm selfish or demanding.

I like to give my partner little clues that I'm unhappy or that I want to do something differently. The problem is my partner almost never picks up the clues.

I try to be considerate of my lover's needs. Even if I feel strongly about something, I'll say, "It's not that important. Whatever you want will be fine with me."

I've spent my whole life being a "nice" person. In relationships I usually give in to what my partner feels strongly about and hope one day my partner will reciprocate and let *me* win a few. But that rarely happens.

The more I give in the more distant and resentful I feel. In the past, I've given in and given in until one day I'm out the door. I'm afraid of that happening again.

Feeling Trapped

Renee's case illustrates the problem many of us have failing to stand up for ourselves in an intimate relationship. An outspoken person where she works, Renee frequently has to be assertive with customers and suppliers. Yet she explains that when she is in love she becomes "so timid and compliant you wouldn't recognize me." When her current boyfriend had his mother visiting him from out of town, he asked Renee to entertain and spend time with his mother every night while he was busy working late. Did Renee say anything to stand up for herself? Of course not.

According to Renee, "At first I couldn't believe what he was asking me to do. Why should I give up all my free time to play hostess to his mother while he pretended to be overworked and avoided her like the plague." Yet as she had done so often in the past, Renee kept quiet and didn't express her concerns. The one time she made an indirect comment in jest that "your mother and I are becoming an item . . . people are beginning to talk," Renee's boyfriend grew silent with a hurt look on his face. She recalls, "He sat there sulking for what seemed an eternity. I figured it was easier to do what he wanted than make him angry with me."

As a result of keeping her anger locked inside from this and several other minor conflicts with her otherwise caring boyfriend, Renee gradually began to feel trapped by the relationship. Like so many others who have trouble saying no or expressing their needs to a romantic partner, Renee was falling out of love and feeling powerless to do anything about it. Quite often, even the best relationships are jeopardized when one or both partners allow unspoken resentments to pile up and block their good feelings for the other person.

When she came to me for advice, I asked Renee to describe what this current situation with her boyfriend reminded her of from the past. Had there ever been a similar experience in which she gave in for fear of disappointing the man in her life and then felt trapped by the relationship?

Thinking back, Renee remembered several times when her former boyfriend had gotten his way by sulking silently just as her current boyfriend had done. Digging deeper, she also recalled, "As a young girl, I can see my father at the dinner table wearing a hurt look on his face whenever he didn't get his way. I used to feel so guilty. Even if I had disagreed with him because he was clearly wrong, I still felt guilty. One time he didn't talk to me for days because I'd challenged him on something and he lost the argument. That really hurt to see him sulking and somehow I thought I was to blame. Gradually I learned it was easier to let him win than to risk hurting his feelings."

Based on her experiences with a sulking father and a former boyfriend who used the same guilt-inducing de-

vices, Renee had developed the habit of silently resenting the men she loved and was outwardly trying to please.
As a result, any relationship she might get involved with
was in danger of becoming a repetition of the same
pattern. The only way Renee could start standing up for
herself and stop feeling distance and distrust for the men
she loved would be to work through her emotional baggage. Not until she overcame her fears of hurting her
father and her former lover could she start communicating to her current boyfriend more honestly and constructively.

"I Never Know Why She Likes Me"

Jeff's case illustrates a different kind of "pleaser" dilemma that affects many people. A handsome and financially successful real estate developer, Jeff nonetheless
feels insecure whenever he is in love because of his fear
that "unless I keep doing things to impress my partner
I'm afraid she's going to lose interest in me."

With his current lover, Jeff describes feeling especially
nervous because, "She's not impressed with the gifts I
buy her or the flowery things I might say to be romantic.
Even though she insists she likes me for who I am, I
don't know if I can trust that. Unless I'm going out of my
way to impress a woman I care about, I never know why
she likes me."

Recently Jeff and his current lover had a bitter argument because of his possessiveness and jealousy. According to Jeff, "We were at a party and there was a man
paying a lot of attention to my girlfriend, who said not to
worry and that I should trust her. But I immediately felt
a sense of panic. Whenever I'm in love, it's only a matter
of time before the woman I care about feels smothered
and walks out. I'm so afraid of being left that I unintentionally make the person want to get away from me. I

don't know how to be with a woman without this fear of being rejected ruining our time together."

Like many pleasers, Jeff grew up with a low sense of self-esteem. He describes his family situation as, "I was the best little boy in the world when I did things that pleased my parents. When I did something for myself which they didn't approve of, I was the worst little boy in the world. There was no middle ground. Either I was showered with gifts and attention or I was devastated with anger and criticism."

As an adult, Jeff is like many pleasers whose fear of being judged by their lovers reminds me of the Groucho Marx line, "I would never join a club that would have me as a member." Jeff can't understand why anyone would stay in a relationship with him unless he bends over backwards and does what his partner wants.

If you are like Jeff and seem to be trying too hard to please your partner, or you're never sure whether you have the right to be yourself, this might be a good time to do some inner work. Where did you learn it was unsafe to ask for what you needed or stand up for yourself with a loved one? When did you get punished or criticized for not living up to someone's expectations? When did you start trying so hard?

No one should remain stuck in the rut of feeling belittled or intimidated by the person you love the most. If relationships cause you to deny yourself and pretend to be an all-giving saint, you need to ask why.

In recent years, support groups have begun to form to help people who find themselves always stuck in the role of the pleaser or the giver. Because of several breakthrough books, including Margaret and Jordan Paul's *Do I Have to Give Up Me to Be Loved By You*, Robin Norwood's *Women Who Love Too Much*, and Susan Forward's *Men Who Hate Women and the Women Who Love Them*, it is no longer a secret that many people feel trapped in painful relationships. Discovering why you become a self-limiting pleaser for other people could mean the start of a healthier way of being in love. You owe it to yourself and those you care about to break out of the habit of keeping your needs locked inside.

"The Demander"

At the opposite end of the spectrum from the pleaser is the demander, a person who becomes extremely critical and bossy whenever he or she is in love. Without knowing why, a demander picks at his or her partner until that partner utters the classic lament heard in so many relationships, "I can't win with this person. No matter what I do it's not good enough."

Just as the pleaser had strong reasons from painful life experiences for being so compliant, so does the demander have strong reasons for being so critical and impatient. Here are some of the things I've heard demanders say to explain why they criticize their partners so readily. How many of these sound like you or your current or former partner?

> I used to be sweet and trusting in relationships. But I've been burned too many times. Now I let my partner know exactly how I feel without any sugar-coating.

> I expect a lot from people. I'm just as hard on myself, so why should I be different with others?

> I have no patience whatsoever. If I tell my partner to do something and then it's not done, what am I supposed to do—ignore it?

> The problem isn't that I'm too demanding. It's that other people are too sensitive.

"I Deserve Better Than This"

Nancy is a successful marketing executive and has two children from a previous marriage. At work she tends to be fairly even-tempered, recognizing that "problems are bound to arise." Yet in relationships, she admits she is "somewhat of a perfectionist. I expect a lot from any man I'm serious about."

Nancy explains why she demands so much: "If a man leads me on with lofty promises and then turns out to be a loser, I get furious. After what I've been through supporting two kids and making it on my own, I know I deserve better than this."

Recently Nancy was introduced by a close friend to a man who not only didn't make lofty promises but showed no signs of being what she calls "a loser." Yet after seeing each other for almost a year and talking about moving in together, Nancy was surprised and upset when he broke off the relationship.

She describes, "He was a decent guy, the first one I've met in a long time. But he said he couldn't stay in a relationship with me because of how much I was determined to criticize, find fault, and be dissatisfied. I don't know why I did it, yet even with this man who had so little wrong with him I was still trying to fix him. Several times we talked about how critical I am and I tried to change. But it's a habit I don't know how to break."

When Nancy and I talked about her earlier relationships with her father and her ex-husband, the reason for her critical and demanding behavior became apparent. Both Nancy's father and her former husband suffered from recurring problems with alcohol and drug addiction. For years Nancy had tried to help them get their lives together again. She resented the fact both men resisted her efforts to help them. She also felt guilty for leaving both her father and her ex-husband when she realized she needed to take better care of herself and her children.

Nancy's problem in relationships was her chronic habit of wanting to fix any man she cared about. Even if someone didn't resemble her father or her ex-husband, she still felt an uncontrollable urge to criticize and "repair" each new lover because she had been so frustrated at being unable to help the first two significant men in her life.

If you were raised with subtle messages that it was your job to rescue or fix a troubled parent or ex-lover, you may still be doing that to the detriment of your adult relationships. If you notice yourself giving too much advice or expecting too much from a loved one who is only human, possibly the problem lies within. Especially if the parent or ex-spouse you couldn't help was alcoholic, drug-addicted, or emotionally unstable, you may still be blaming yourself and wanting to amend a situation that wasn't your fault. Each of us needs to learn that in certain cases we must simply love someone while accepting that we can't change them.

In Nancy's case, learning to accept the vulnerabilities of her partner and not wanting to make everything better was a huge breakthrough. Two years after she began working through her unresolved issues from the past, she met another man who was neither "a loser" nor someone who needed very much "repair." Nancy admits, "There was still a tiny part of me that wanted to change him, mold him, and demand he become everything I've ever wanted in a man. Yet I caught myself and remembered to love him and enjoy him as he is. As a result, we're doing pretty well together. For the first time in my life, I'm actually appreciating my partner's imperfections."

"I Don't Know Why I Get So Angry"

Walter's case illustrates a different aspect of "The Demander." A soft-spoken and caring personnel director for a health-care facility, Walter doesn't appear to be a demanding type of person. Yet in his marriage, Walter occasionally finds himself yelling at his wife and children over the smallest disagreements.

He admits, "I don't know why I get so angry. I come home from work expecting things to be relaxed and pleasant around the house, but then my wife and I get into an argument over something and I start to fly off the handle. Or my kids are acting up and I hear myself screaming at them the way I promised myself I'd never do, especially since I grew up in a family where everyone dreaded my father's temper tantrums. Now I've started to resemble that kind of bully and I don't like what I see."

Like many demanders, Walter issues ultimatums and criticizes his loved ones not because he's an insensitive brute but because of something he doesn't know how to control. Fortunately, Walter came for counseling, as he began to realize, "The longer I put off doing something about my outbursts and tantrums around the house, the more I began to jeopardize my marriage and my closeness with my children. When I looked into their eyes and saw they were afraid of me, I knew it was time to find out what was going on."

If you or the person you live with is a soft-spoken and caring individual much of the time, but prone to outbursts of blind rage on occasion, it's important to uncover the reasons why. None of us wants to mistreat our loved ones or be mistreated by a spouse or lover. Yet if the tantrums and explosions are not addressed, it can turn your home life into a living hell.

What Walter discovered in our sessions together is that

he, like many people, never learned how to express anger in a safe and appropriate way. His only role models were either people who stuffed their anger tightly inside or who blew up in angry outbursts from the smallest provocations. Gradually over a period of months, Walter learned how to ask for what he needed around the house without attacking or criticizing his loved ones. Instead of assuming he had the right to demand respect, he began to recognize the importance of earning and maintaining his family's respect.

Most importantly, Walter learned what many hardworking people need to recognize—that bringing home a load of unresolved anger and frustration from the office each day can be hazardous to your relationship. We each need to find ways to unwind at the end of a stressful day without turning our tensions on our loved ones. Walter began experimenting with healthier ways to let off steam—long walks, meditation, aerobics, and a nightly discussion in which both he and his wife talked about their day for five minutes each without interruption. As with many couples, Walter and his wife discovered that it's a lot easier to be in love when you're handling your stresses well than if you're walking around like a time bomb about to explode.

How to Make Changes in Your Relationship

Once you recognize something needs to be improved in your romantic partnership, how do you bring up the problem without angering or alienating your loved one? Quite often one or both partners know exactly what needs to be done to save a troubled relationship, yet the words they choose and the tactics they employ only lead to nasty arguments.

For example:

> Both Jean and Caroline know they want to improve the way in which chores and financial decisions are handled in their relationship. Yet when Jean brings up the subject, Caroline gets defensive. When Caroline brings up the subject, Jean gets defensive. As a result, chores and financial issues continue to be an unsolved conflict area that slowly tears away at their love for each other.

What can you do to improve the way you and your loved one communicate about difficult issues such as your different desires in lovemaking, your conflicting ideas about raising children, or your opposing ideas on certain political issues? How do you resolve the fights and power struggles that arise sooner or later in every intimate relationship?

Based on my experience working with hundreds of couples—heterosexuals, gays, lesbians, married couples, cohabiting partners, and those living apart—I've discovered an interesting pattern. Most partners are attracted to each other because of what they have in common but eventually their relationship becomes a battle zone because of what they *don't* have in common.

Think about your own relationships, both current and past. What happened when your way of doing something clashed with your partner's like a bug hitting the windshield at sixty miles an hour? What happened when you said *potayto* and your partner said *potahto*? Or when you said *tomayto* and your partner said *tomahto*? Did you feel like calling the whole thing off?

If you tend to be the pleaser and let your partner win most of the battles, what do you do with the resentments that begin to accumulate inside your emotions? Certainly there has to be a better way of resolving your differences than if you keep backing down and pretending you're happy about something which you know deep inside isn't what you want.

If you tend to be the demander and find yourself using guilt, intimidation, and self-righteous sermons to try to get your way, do you recognize the costs of that strategy? Your partner may give in and make it look like you've won, but in fact you may have lost because your partner slowly begins to resent you for your nasty methods of doing battle.

Learning to fight fair is essential if your relationship is going to grow and improve. Yet most couples either don't fight at all, or they fight with as much reasonableness as two five-year-olds quarreling over a sandbox shovel.

Do You Fight Fair?

One of the biggest improvements most couples need to make in their relationship is to learn how to argue in a way that doesn't lead to leftover resentments. Knowing the fine art of fighting fair with a loved one is important in the early stages as well as the later stages of a relationship. Couples who can address their dissatisfactions and still feel good about each other wind up enjoying a long, healthy partnership. The vast majority, who fight with nasty tactics such as using guilt and intimidation, usually wind up hating each other or splitting apart.

There are several reasons why it's so hard for most people to fight fair in a loving relationship. Here are some of the ones I hear most often:

> I start out being reasonable but pretty soon I sense that I want to *win*. Even if I'm partially at fault, I won't admit it because I don't want to give my partner a chance to feel anything less than extremely guilty.

> Our problem is that we both want so badly to avoid any arguments or tensions that we keep things inside until

they start to sneak out in nasty little sarcastic remarks. It's the sarcasm and slow-boiling tempers that are making us feel so distant from each other, not the fights.

With us it always comes as a surprise when we have one of our big screaming matches. We'll be going along great for a few weeks or even a few months and then boom—some petty issue gets both of us so self-righteous we can't hear what the other person is saying.

These individuals are not the only ones who lose their common sense when a dispute breaks out with a lover or spouse. We all have our moments when we seem to forget everything except the unkind words a romantic partner has just hurled in our direction.

It takes great courage and inner wisdom to be able to catch yourself in the middle of becoming self-righteous or manipulative. Instead of trying to win a lover's quarrel by fighting dirty, you might want to stop and ask yourself, "Do I really need to be so manipulative? Do I want to win this battle only to hurt the relationship? Or is there a better way to resolve this disagreement so that both sides feel heard, understood, and appreciated?"

The Twenty-Minute Time-Out

Here's a powerful technique you can use whenever you are in a nasty argument with a loved one or whenever you start to notice yourself becoming defensive, manipulative or self-righteous. I call it the "Twenty-Minute Time-Out" and it has worked wonders for many couples, not only to resolve tensions but also to prevent harmful divisions in a relationship.

This is how it works:

1. If an argument with a loved one is bringing out the angry child within each of you, don't keep attacking each other. Stop the argument long enough to remember this

is not a life-or-death struggle for control. Instead of continuing to view each other as "the enemy," one of you needs to call a Twenty-Minute Time-Out. You might say, "I need a short time-out, maybe twenty minutes or so, to find out what's keeping us from understanding each other." Or you can say, "Let's both take twenty minutes to absorb what's been said. Otherwise we'll both keep talking and not listening to each other."

2. If your partner objects or says, "We've got to work this out together right now. We can't take a break," don't get defensive. Simply explain, "We *are* going to work this out together. But first I need to unwind and start hearing what you've been saying. The best way to do that is to have twenty minutes apart and then we'll get back together."

3. During your twenty minutes alone, be sure to notice your breathing. Take deep breaths, in and out, as you let your feelings come up and your tensions unwind. You may want to pound a mattress, scream into a sweater or pillow, take a brisk walk, or write in your journal to release your current anger and break out of the defensive rut you might be in.

4. Most importantly, you should avoid the natural temptation to use the twenty minutes to buttress your argument or plan a new way of getting the other person to admit he or she is wrong and you are right. That's not what the Twenty-Minute Time-Out is for! It's not so you can become more defensive or self-righteous. Rather, this is an opportunity to start seeing both sides of the issue and remembering that it takes two to tango. If you keep noticing that your mind is blaming the other person and calling you 100 percent innocent, stop this train of thought and ask yourself these questions:

> What was my contribution to the problem? What haven't I admitted to my partner (and possibly to myself) that I tend to do which brings on this disagreement?

Why am I afraid to admit my contribution to the problem? What would happen if I owned up to what I do in situations like these so we can look at how to prevent future arguments on the same subject?

Why am I afraid to accept what my partner is saying or admit that I see some validity in this other point of view? What would happen if I saw both sides of the issue?

Please note that if you admit your contribution to the problem, it doesn't mean you are taking all the blame. It's an invitation to communicate, rather than a confrontation to alienate. Until both sides can admit their part in creating the problem you both share, nothing constructive will be accomplished. Hopefully you will not have to be alone in admitting that you helped bring on the problem. If your partner refuses to admit his or her part, you might want to say, "I also need to hear that you know this problem comes from both of us. I've begun to understand what I bring to the situation. I need to hear what you think you bring as well."

5. During the Time-Out, you may want to look within and uncover what unresolved issues from the past this current fight has retriggered. When did you have a similar experience in your family or a previous relationship? What happened then to prevent you from resolving your hurt feelings or getting your needs met? What do you need now to make sure the hurt isn't going to be repeated again?

When the twenty minutes are over, you may want to describe the previous hurt to your partner—not as an attack but as a request for support and understanding. For example, you might come out at the end of twenty minutes and say, "I think I understand now why this issue is so upsetting to me. I need your support as I explain something that happened a long time ago but which might be affecting the problem we're working on now."

6. In some instances, you may still feel tense or unclear after twenty minutes of quiet time alone. In that case, you might want to talk over the problem with a counselor or support group who can help you uncover deeper layers of understanding. In the meantime, you can return to your partner and do your best to hear what he or she is saying, while remembering that both of you have the right to your feelings on this issue. As soon as you both stop trying to convince each other that one side is right and the other side is wrong, the argument will be headed toward a healthy resolution.

This Twenty-Minute Time-Out exercise can be a relationship-saver. Instead of letting arguments go on for hours or days, you can break the vicious cycle of accusations and rebuttals by taking twenty minutes of uninterrupted time to unwind and relax. Instead of denying your anger with a dishonest, "I'm fine. I'm not upset," the Twenty-Minute Time-Out helps you get to the reasons behind the argument. Rather than attacking and hurting each other, it gives you a chance to start seeing both points of view. For example, here is a case that illustrates why couples drift apart and how an exercise like the Twenty-Minute Time-Out can help them unravel their struggle before it splits them apart forever.

"It's Not That I'm Too Critical . . . It's That He's So Defensive"

Alicia and Keith have been together for almost four years in what Alicia describes as a relationship that "began with great passion and excitement but has turned into a struggle of wills." She explains, "When Keith and I first met, the closeness and warmth were incredible. I had never enjoyed sex very much with previous partners, but with Keith it was completely different. He was so patient, so gentle, and so romantic. The first time we made love I felt a sense of complete surrender and tears came to my eyes. I never thought I could love anyone that much."

Alicia continues, "I knew it couldn't always be like that, but I never expected us to become the way we are now. These days when Keith wants to make love, I feel hesitant, resentful, turned off. Something has definitely changed between us sexually, even though we're still close in most other areas."

While Keith agrees with much of what Alicia says about their relationship, he sees the change in their sex life quite differently. According to Keith, "She's right about the fact we were incredibly passionate and tender at the beginning. But she's leaving out the most important part. Alicia can be very critical and short-tempered, especially about sex. Nowadays when we try to make love, she doesn't relax or let me love her. She's always got something she doesn't like, some criticism she has to give with a sarcastic tone that makes me feel frustrated and angry. I still want to be close to her but it's impossible when she's so uptight."

Alicia disagrees. "The problem," she explains, "is not that I'm too critical. It's that he's so defensive. All I do is ask for what I want, or tell him not to do something I don't want, and he goes crazy. You say one word to Keith and he thinks you're being a bitch. Even if you say it nicely, he reacts like you've just challenged his whole sense of manhood. I can't relax or feel sexual with someone who's that defensive."

Ironically, Keith and Alicia are not alone in having this problem. It's very common for both the person making suggestions about sex and the person receiving advice about it to feel tense and defensive. Most couples have trouble talking about things they like or dislike in bed. Those insecurities are compounded when one or both partners react with anger and defensiveness to the slightest bit of advice.

I encouraged Alicia and Keith to break their vicious cycle of attacking and resenting each other by explaining to them how to use the Twenty-Minute Time-Out exercise described earlier. Quite often in a sexual argument or in any other anxious dispute, the only way to stop aggravating the problem is to take a Time-Out and look at what's underneath the current miscommunication.

The next time Alicia and Keith began to criticize each other and felt as if they were in a battle, they tried the Twenty-Minute Time-Out. For Alicia, the technique gave her the chance to find out why Keith's defensiveness was so hard for her to take. When she relaxed and asked herself, "What does this situation remind me of from the past?," she recalled several times in her life when she had been criticized simply for expressing her likes and dislikes in a nonthreatening manner.

Alicia explains, "All my life when I've asserted myself and said what I wanted or didn't want I've gotten flack for it. Especially with the men in my life, including my Dad and several of my bosses. When I would say in a nice way, 'This isn't working for me' or 'I don't like that,' they would get defensive and angry. I wasn't trying to hurt their feelings or threaten their masculinity. But as soon as I made a contradictory remark, I could feel their anger. So gradually I learned to keep my mouth shut."

In her relationship with Keith, Alicia had decided that lovemaking was too important to keep silent when Keith did something she didn't like. She describes how she thought that "if he loved me he'd want to hear what feels good and what doesn't. It's so hard for me to ask for what I want in the first place, especially about something like lovemaking. But then when I do finally get up the courage and tell him what I enjoy and what I don't, all I get in return is his anger and defensiveness. It makes me crazy. So I either keep it to myself or I make my point with a little bit of sarcasm."

Now that Alicia understood some of the reasons why these sexual arguments were so difficult for her, she asked the second question that helps make the Twenty-Minute Time-Out so powerful an exercise. Even though she was pretty sure the problem was Keith's fault, she followed the instructions and asked herself, "What is my contribution to the problem?"

At first, Alicia wasn't sure. But then when she thought about what she might be doing to aggravate the situation, she realized her sarcasm was probably not a very effective way to make her feelings known. By the end of the twenty minutes, Alicia had stopped blaming Keith for the entire problem and begun to see that her own struggle to communicate was an important part of the potential solution.

When Keith began his twenty minutes alone, he had trouble relaxing or following the instructions. Like many of us, Keith found it was much easier to blame his partner than look within at what he might be contributing to the arguments. Only when he remembered to breathe slowly in and out did his mind stop criticizing Alicia and start looking deeper for a solution. After several minutes of relaxing and unwinding, Keith was finally ready to begin asking himself questions that might reveal some constructive answers.

The first question Keith asked was, "Why am I having so much trouble hearing Alicia's suggestions? Where did I learn to be so defensive?" As I had suggested to him during one of our sessions together, "The more specific you make the questions, the easier it is to start looking within for solutions." I had advised Keith not to settle for generalized questions such as, "What does this issue remind me of?," but to dig deeper with questions like, "Why am I having so much trouble hearing this person's point of view? Where did I learn to be so defensive?"

Reflecting back to his upbringing and his early family relationships, Keith began to think of some reasons why he was so quick to get angry with Alicia. He explained later, "I don't want to be closed off to Alicia when she tells me what she doesn't like in bed, but when you look at the way I was raised in my family it begins to make sense. I had three older sisters who used to boss me around a lot. And since I was the first male child in the family, I got a lot of pressure put on me from both of my parents to do everything right and make all their dreams come true.

"Living with all those expectations on my shoulders made me resent whenever someone says, 'You're not doing this good enough.' I put so much pressure on myself that I have trouble when someone adds to that pressure from outside. Especially when the comments come from a woman, who probably reminds me of my sisters and my Mom. I know it's not fair to Alicia, but it's hard for me to change this overnight."

Now that both Alicia and Keith recognized how their miscommunication in bed had a lot more to do with issues from long ago than with their love for each other, it was easier to begin working on the problem together. Alicia knew that from her side it was important that she catch herself whenever she started to make sarcastic remarks. Keith realized that from his side it was important to catch himself whenever he started to think Alicia was putting him down with her justified reactions to their lovemaking.

In addition, because of their discussions following the Twenty-Minute Time-Out, Keith began to understand how hard it is for Alicia to express her wants and needs, especially in light of her bad experiences with men who got angry with her simply for having an opinion. Alicia began to understand how hard it is for Keith to hear feedback without thinking it's a personal attack that he's not good enough.

Knowing more about each other helped Keith and Alicia begin the slow process of rebuilding the trust and comfort that had been eroded by their constant sexual arguments. Yet gradually, over a period of months, they began to enjoy their lovemaking again. As Alicia describes, "Knowing what each of us needs in order to feel safe with one another has brought us a lot closer. When we make love now, it's even more exciting than during the passionate early days of the relationship. In addition, there's a deeper level of caring that I can feel when we embrace."

Are You Ready to Reveal Yourself to Your Partner?

In some relationships, the partners become more guarded and distant as the years go by. In other relationships, the ones that grow and become more fulfilling, the partners work through layer after layer of defensiveness from the past until they discover the tremendous happiness of really loving and being loved by another person.

Working through barriers caused by hurts from long ago doesn't mean there's something wrong with your relationship. It means you and your loved one have the good sense to know that what you've built together is too important to let it be ruined by unfinished business from the past.

Many couples are surprised and upset when issues from the past reappear as conflicts to resolve. Some ask, "How could this be happening to us? I never thought *we'd* be having problems." Yet if you take each difficulty in the relationship and turn it into an opportunity to learn more about yourself and the person you are with, it will help your love grow stronger and more enduring.

Instead of reacting with shock or anger when issues from the past show up in your love life, remember to go back and apply the "Four Levels of Letting Go" (described on pages 00–00). If you or your partner have some unspoken hurts from childhood or early relationships, now is a good time to start healing them so your current love can be successful. If you or your partner still has some unfinished business with an ex-spouse or ex-lover, cleaning up those issues can dramatically improve the here-and-now relationship.

Finding and building a satisfying relationship can be one of the most important and rewarding challenges of your life. Yet in those angry moments when you and your loved one are both arguing without listening, you need to stop and remember to use a technique such as the Twenty-Minute Time-Out. You now have the tools necessary to identify and resolve the issues that can split you apart. Don't forget to use these tools while your love for each other still has a chance to survive and flourish!

Working Through Your Mixed Feelings About Work

4

> In order that people may be happy
> in their work, these three things
> are needed: they must be fit for
> it. They must not do too much of
> it. And they must have a sense of
> success in it.
>
> —John Ruskin

Have you noticed how many people these days are working more and enjoying it less? Maybe one of those people is you.

Quite often we change companies, job titles, or even organizer notebooks in order to feel better about what we do from nine to five. Yet a short time later the same dissatisfactions and unresolved questions arise. When your commute is an hour late, when your boss is in one of those moods, or when your hard work is wasted because of a miscommunication, do you sometimes ask yourself:

Is this what I really want to be doing on a daily basis?

Why am I pushing myself this hard and still not receiving what I deserve?

Why am I surrounded by so many difficult people?

Is there any way I could enjoy my work more than I do now?

Whether you currently are employed, unemployed, working for others, or working for yourself, you may feel as though you're stuck in a rut. Months and years pass without things getting much better. Is it the job? Is it the people? Is it something you carry inside from long ago?

Here is a brief quiz that will help you uncover some of the things you might want to resolve about your work life. Answer each question honestly; there are no right or wrong answers.

1. When people ask what you do for a living, do you

   (a) Feel good about your answer.
   (b) Start explaining and justifying why you do what you do.
   (c) Resent them for asking.

2. When you hear of a friend or relative who is making a lot of money, do you

   (a) Feel glad because he or she has earned it.
   (b) Start questioning why you aren't earning more.
   (c) Feel angry about the disappointments you've suffered.

3. When you think back to your career aspirations as a teenager and young adult, do you

   (a) Feel you've done as well or better than you planned.
   (b) Find yourself filled with regrets and frustrations.
   (c) Think about the people who've let you down or disrupted your progress.

4. When you have to deal with a certain difficult person at work, do you

(a) Understand how to manage this person reasonably well.

(b) Feel bottled up with anger at how much he or she gets on your nerves.

(c) Feel like quitting so you won't have to deal with this person any longer.

5. If you inherited or won enough money to support yourself and your loved ones the rest of your life, would you

(a) Keep doing the same kind of work you are doing now.

(b) Switch to something different, such as _____.

(c) Do as little as possible.

6. When you think about what you'd like to be doing in five years, do you

(a) Feel you're right on schedule or moving toward that goal.

(b) Worry that your plans might not come true.

(c) Regret that no clear picture comes to mind.

7. When pressures from work start to wear you down, do you

(a) Know how to lighten your load effectively.

(b) Feel powerless and unable to catch up or relax.

(c) Resent the rut you've fallen into.

Note: If you checked (b) or (c) more than (a), you would be kidding yourself if you said you didn't need to make some improvements in your work situation. Now might be a good time to start examining why your livelihood feels anything but lively.

Where Do You Begin?

There are three different ways to resolve your mixed feelings about work. One is to examine whether you are fit for your job—if it suits your personality, interests and sense of purpose in life. If you are going to work each day at a job that doesn't feel like you, it's no wonder you are plagued with misgivings.

The second area to examine is whether you are overworked. Too many people who love their jobs start to resent their bosses, their assignments, or their co-workers if the work load becomes too much. If you find yourself frequently exhausted, stressed, or short-tempered, or if you start noticing physical symptoms of overwork (back, stomach, head, and muscle aches or heart trouble, high blood pressure and nervous tensions), you may need to reexamine why you might be working yourself to death.

The third area to look at is whether you feel a sense of success in your work. I'm not talking about success in the sense of making a zillion dollars and retiring by age thirty. Rather, I am referring to the sense of satisfaction that your work is meaningful, that you do it well, that it challenges you to grow, and that you feel sufficiently acknowledged and rewarded for your contribution. If you don't feel your job is giving you what you need, it's hard to feel resolved about the direction your life is taking.

Part One:
Does Your Job Fit Who You Are?

If you are like most people, you were raised with the belief that you can't expect to find a job that suits your personality and interests. Especially if your parents grew up in hard times, the notion was passed down to you that "A job is a job. It's a way to bring home money and you can't expect it to be enjoyable or meaningful."

Yet I don't have to tell you a job is much more than a job. It's something that occupies a huge percentage of your lifetime. It's an opportunity to explore your talents, creativity, interpersonal skills and personal goals. It's a chance to make an impact and do something worthwhile with your life.

Despite the security-oriented fears that many of us grew up with, we all know there are people who left a secure position that felt wrong to them and discovered a more rewarding job that not only felt right but proved to be an excellent career move. Even if the new job wasn't perfect or took a long time to come to fruition, there is great satisfaction in doing something you enjoy every day rather than simply getting by at something you detest.

Before you can even begin to look for or create the job that fits your unique traits, however, you need to unravel the emotional obstacles that tell you it's "selfish," "impractical," or "unrealistic" to be looking for a livelihood that feels close to who you are. Only when you understand why you have believed you can't have what you want can you begin exploring how to make what you want into a reality.

For example, Laurence was active in political causes during high school and college, yet when he graduated and entered the work world he accepted his parents' belief that you can't be too choosy about how to make your living. Getting married soon after college, Laurence decided his first priority was to make a secure income. While he knew he was a "people person" and wanted to work in personnel or management, he didn't think it mattered what kind of company he worked for. So when he was hired by a large aerospace company to work in their human resources department, Laurence took the offer.

During several years of climbing the corporate ladder and becoming a well-paid middle-manager for the aerospace firm, Laurence felt increasingly dissatisfied with his work. He didn't like the fact that he was employed by a weapons manufacturer and was helping to escalate the arms race. He didn't enjoy spending most of his time surrounded by engineers and computer specialists with whom he had little in common. In addition, he kept wondering if his talents for working with people were being underutilized. Since he was in a large corporation, most of Laurence's time was spent not solving human problems but filling out paperwork—preparing budgets, company policy, flow charts, and changes in organizational structures.

Eventually Laurence began to show physical symptoms to go with his emotional dissatisfactions. A skin flare-up on his back got worse despite the medications suggested by several physicians. Recurring headaches made him sluggish and short-tempered when he was home each night with his wife and two children.

Although he finally sought counseling for his problem, Laurence was sure he couldn't let go of the secure career path he had worked so hard to maintain. He admitted, "I have to remember I'm lucky to be in a secure position like this. I can't just throw it all away and start over at the bottom somewhere else."

Like many people who knowingly or unknowingly adopted the fears, expectations, and values of their parents' generation, Laurence couldn't find out what was right for him until he started thinking for himself. What were his own interests, values, talents and preferences? What options did he have that might not have existed when his parents were his age? What jobs would feel more like him and less like selling out?

When Laurence dealt with these questions, he realized how much he had held back the most special aspects of his personality in order to fit into a work environment that felt compromising. He explains, "I thought I had no choice but to be one kind of person with my friends and my wife while I was a completely different person at work. I thought I had no alternative but to keep my values and my insights silent while I pretended to be just like the others in my department. I'm an expert at faking it, but there's only so long you can pretend before the deception starts to take its toll on your spirit."

I asked Laurence to make a list of the hidden beliefs he would be violating if he left his current job and found something that was more satisfying and heartfelt. On his list, Laurence described:

> If I leave a secure job, it will prove my parents were right when they said I'm selfish and impractical.

> If I take a cut in salary, it will mean I'm not a good provider or a caring husband and father.

> If I leave this job and find the next one isn't all that great, my wife and my friends will know I'm a flake.

> If I go to work somewhere else, how will I know I'm not going to get fired, laid off, or wind up in an industry that's going through a slump?

> If I don't stay at my current job, I might lose out on the health plan and pension benefits they have here.

When Laurence and I then began to brainstorm about various career options he might explore, he cautiously admitted he had a strong preference for one particular line of work. What Laurence had always wanted to do but had never felt the freedom to try is become a schoolteacher. He imagined he would enjoy working with young children, would be good at coming up with creative lesson plans and teaching devices, and would finally be able to put his interpersonal skills to good use. Yet he'd never taken this desire seriously. Years ago he'd been told repeatedly he shouldn't become a teacher because it wasn't macho enough, it didn't pay enough, it might mean working in a rough neighborhood, and it was viewed by society as less prestigious than many other fields.

Like so many of us, Laurence was holding back his own enthusiasm for something he imagined he might enjoy because it didn't meet other people's expectations of him. So often I work with people who come into counseling with an unspoken idea of what they want. Yet they stop short of their goals because they don't want to make waves or face the fears and limiting beliefs they were given long ago by parents, society, or painful past experiences.

Even though there had been news items recently about the fact that there were numerous openings in the city school system, for Laurence the decision to leave the corporate world and go into teaching wasn't an easy one. He and his wife had to adjust to a 30 percent cut in his salary. Laurence had to attend evening courses to qualify for his teaching credentials. He had to learn to cope with the stresses, demands, and frustrations that make teaching a highly challenging field.

Yet after a difficult first year, Laurence began to feel he'd made the right choice. He describes the difference as follows, "I'm so much more involved in what I do now. There's a stronger sense of wanting to do a good job and not feeling like I'm wearing a mask or pretending I care about petty issues that used to occupy my time in my old job. I feel rewarded by even the smallest impact I have on these kids. Sometimes I still hear occasional doubts running through my mind that I should be earning more or doing something that's closer to the expectations I was raised with. But nothing beats the satisfaction of helping a young boy or girl develop skills and feel good about themselves."

If you are like Laurence and think you might be working in the wrong type of job for your particular interests, personality or talents, you may want to talk to a career counselor or pick up one of the helpful career-change books available in most bookstores and libraries. I've seen people make successful career changes in their twenties, thirties, forties, fifties, sixties, and seventies. It's never too late to let go of something you were doing to meet other people's expectations and to start building something that comes from your heart. Even if you have to begin slowly or take on a second job to make your plans come to fruition, the rewards of working each day at something you care about are enormous.

What If Staying at Your Job Is the Right Decision?

In many cases you don't have to change jobs or careers to resolve a dissatisfying situation at work. Quite often a much smaller change in the way you relate to your work or the people around you can bring about dramatic results. For instance, if a certain supervisor or co-worker has been driving you crazy and making you want to quit your job, there may be an effective resolution that doesn't require you sacrifice all you've put into this job or career path. Instead of running from the situation, it might be better to look within and see what kind of emotional baggage your conflict with this person has reactivated.

In many work conflicts, the problem is likely to be that your boss or co-workers fit too closely to an unresolved pattern you had with a difficult person from long ago. The person who is driving you crazy on the job probably reminds you of someone you can't stand from the past. Maybe your tyrannical boss reminds you of a belittling parent or sibling who used to make you feel small. Possibly a jealous or back-stabbing co-worker reminds you of someone who betrayed you long ago. Most likely a personality clash you are having with someone in your current job is similar to a personality clash you had growing up in your family or in previous work situations.

For example, Roseanne has been thinking about quitting her job and possibly changing careers because of an ongoing battle with her boss. A hardworking administrator at a health-related agency, Roseanne is the one person her boss and co-workers rely on during a crunch. According to Roseanne, "Whenever things get piled up around here, everyone assumes they can pass their dirty work over to me. Especially my boss, who looks to me whenever he needs help but turns to others when he's giving out praise or benefits."

Roseanne's dissatisfaction with her job came to a head a few weeks earlier when she stayed at work until seven o'clock one evening handling a series of crises. Roseanne recalls, "My boss had left at three because he had to pick up one of his children from school. He and his wife are in the process of getting divorced and competing over who's the better parent. Meanwhile, at the office I covered for him and found out the next day he's arranging for a grant for two of my co-workers to do some research that I happen to think is pointless. Last year when I talked to my boss about getting a grant for one of my pet projects, he told me simply I was too busy to take on 'pie-in-the-sky' research."

Like many people who are in conflict with a supervisor or peer at work, Roseanne had a list of legitimate gripes. However, she also had a recurring pattern of feeling overworked and unacknowledged in each of the four positions she'd held in her career. The conflict with her current boss was not the first time she'd felt slighted and resentful. Nor was this the first time she'd felt like quitting a job or changing careers because others were taking her for granted.

To help her get to the root of her pattern, I asked Roseanne if her current situation with her boss resembled anything from before she started her career. After thinking for a moment, Roseanne replied that nothing similar came to mind. Then I asked her to tell me if anyone else from long ago had ever taken her for granted or been like her bosses in not appreciating her hard work.

That question triggered a rush of emotions for Roseanne. With tears in her eyes, she described her anger at being the one person in her family who did the most work and yet received the least amount of affection. According to Roseanne, "Since I was the eldest of three children, it was my job to take care of my younger siblings. Then when my parents got divorced, I wound up taking care of my mother as well. I became her confidante and did all the things around the house she was too busy to do. Yet she still treated my younger brother and sister as her favorites. The more I did for her, the more she took me for granted."

As in so many cases, the very trait that was Roseanne's strength—her ability to work hard and care for others— was also the trait that brought back painful memories of being taken for granted in her family. Quite often the habits we are encouraged for in our families become the skills we use in our careers. Someone who played the role of therapist or mediator in their family often becomes a counselor, social worker, or health-care professional as an adult. While on the one hand this person may enjoy helping others, he or she might also feel resentful at always being expected to take care of others at his or her own expense.

Just as Roseanne was both drawn to and resentful of the role she was asked to play in her family as confidante, nurturer, and helper, so was she filled with mixed emotions about her adult job situations that had similar responsibilities. When bosses came to rely on her the same way her family had, Roseanne found herself reliving in her work life the same feelings of being overworked, taken for granted and unappreciated that she experienced in her family. Just as her parents' divorce had forced her to work extra hard with little acknowledgement, so was her boss' divorce now causing her to take on additional responsibilities that brought back painful memories.

The challenge for Roseanne, or for anyone else who finds he or she is repeatedly falling into traps that are just like an earlier family role, is to understand the pattern in order to stop duplicating it. Until Roseanne sorted out the reasons why she was drawn to situations in which she was overworked and insufficiently appreciated, she would keep finding bosses and co-workers who would take advantage of her in these same ways. Only if she worked through her mixed feelings about working so hard for others would she be ready to break the pattern and find healthier and more satisfying roles to play.

Over a period of months, Roseanne initiated several positive steps to improve the work situation she had resented for many years. First, she used the exercises in Chapter Two in order to work through her resentments toward her boss and toward the members of her family who took her for granted. Next, she resolved to become more aware of any current or future situation that fell into the same pattern of others expecting too much of her and taking her hard work for granted. Then she began to look at ways she could be more assertive and foster more respect and appreciation from bosses and co-workers.

Even though it was hard at first for Roseanne to begin standing up for herself and saying no to things others wanted to dump in her lap, she eventually learned she could do it as well as anyone else. As she describes, "I've learned how to manage my boss so that he knows not to expect me to cover for him every time he's got something better to do. He's gradually learning that I need consideration and acknowledgment as much as anyone else. If he wants me to stay with the agency, he knows he's going to have to fight for the grants I care about. Last week at an important meeting he actually backed me up during a heated discussion of next year's goals for the agency. I'm sure he'll still get on my nerves every now and then, but at least I'm winning more battles than I'm losing these days."

As Roseanne's case illustrates, dealing with power struggles and personality clashes at work is never easy. There are truly difficult bosses, co-workers, and customers who get under our skin from time to time. You and I probably have known more than our share.

Yet when a difficult person disrupts our entire sense of satisfaction with our work or keeps us awake at night with arguments in our heads, something more is happening. We need to look at who this person reminds us of and how we can release our stored anger from the past to become less agitated or victimized by the present situation. When you successfully identify the connection between the present and past, you are well on your way to working through even the most difficult interpersonal conflicts. No one has the right to make your work situation miserable. If someone attempts to do so, you now have the tools to resolve your internal concerns in order to deal with that person more creatively and effectively.

Part Two:
Are You Working Too Hard? ·

Another common reason why people feel alienated and unhappy with their work life is not that they are in the wrong jobs but that they don't know how to slow down or enjoy what they do for a living. Too many people spend more time worrying about the ups and downs of their work than appreciating what's going right. Most ambitious people fall in love with the adrenaline rush of working too hard and then wonder why they feel burned out.

Sometimes people who are pushing themselves too hard don't know it until a loved one or estranged child walks out the door, saying, "Sorry, but you didn't have any time for me." Many people remain unaware of their workaholic tendencies until a heart attack, ulcer, back spasm, or other stress-related symptom makes it painfully evident.

Yet for many of us, even if we know we're working too hard or worrying too much, we might not see any realistic option for letting up. How do you lighten your load without a decrease in your income or someone else passing you by? Are there less drastic alternatives than working yourself to death or dropping out to live like a monk?

If you sincerely want to enjoy your work life and achieve a sense of balance, you will need to come to terms with the rush/collapse/rush/collapse pattern that plagues many successful people today. Here are some of the early warning signs that you or someone you know might be suffering from the most widespread addiction of the decade—becoming a workaholic. Which of the following sound like you?

1. Doing three things at once and then getting mad when someone you love suggests you are working too hard.

2. Worrying so much about failing or making a mistake that you forget to notice your own strengths and accomplishments.

3. Solving a difficult task and then, instead of acknowledging your accomplishment or taking a rest, you go immediately to the next difficult task.

4. Refusing to delegate work to others because you don't want to let go of control.

5. Being so keyed up from your work you can't relax even late at night or on the weekend.

6. Feeling anxious that something is going to fall apart if you take a vacation or slow down.

7. Noticing that when a loved one is talking to you, your thoughts are distracted by unresolved issues from work.

8. Feeling guilty that you aren't spending enough time with your children, family, or friends because of the demands of your job.

9. Always feeling behind in your work and fearing you'll never catch up.

10. Barely remembering the last time you felt rested, relaxed, or alert without artificial stimulants.

Ironically, for most people today, admitting you are a workaholic is no longer an embarrassment. In fact, many individuals point with pride to their battle scars from their obsession with their jobs. In the office you frequently hear two co-workers boasting about who stayed later the night before. In a job interview you might hear the applicant boast, "I'm very driven; everyone tells me I'm a workaholic." On a commuter train you might see two rivals assessing who is bringing the largest pile of work home. In the executive washroom, some workaholics bring their calculators and computer printouts into the stalls so that no time will be lost.

Many people who are working themselves to death laugh at the suggestion they ought to slow down. They'd prefer to offer rationalizations that they have it under control. In the film *The Big Chill*, there's a revealing line about which is more important to many people today— sex or rationalizations? One character says it must be sex but the other replies, "When was the last time you went for a week without a rationalization?"

Once upon a time, I used to think the reason people worked so hard and look so frenetic was because there was so much work to be done. Talking to workaholics in depth I found there is something more that drives us harder than our bodies or our creativity can handle. Sure, there's a lot of work to be done, but something deeper is causing the inner turmoil and constant tension many people experience in their daily lives.

As you read these self-disclosures from women and men who are not so different from you or me, see how many reveal something about the reasons why you or a loved one might be pushing yourselves too hard:

> If I'm insecure about whether or not I can do a difficult project, I sometimes work twice as hard as necessary to cover up those anxious feelings. It's as though I'm telling myself, "See, if I suffer enough you can't say I didn't try."

> I often overwork because I don't want anyone to know how reluctant I am to work at all. I must be so terrified of my own laziness that I go to the opposite extreme to prove how motivated and industrious I am.

> Ever since I got burned by a situation in which I lost nearly everything several years ago, I find myself overreacting to the smallest things that go wrong. I'm so worried about another financial setback that I'm driving my spouse and my employees crazy by breathing down their necks.

> My problem is that I schedule things too closely together. If one appointment gets delayed, all my com-

mitments topple like a row of dominoes. At this point, it's an automatic habit. I fill up my time so tightly because I know if I have gaps between appointments there's this nagging voice in the back of my head that whispers, "Shouldn't you be doing more?"

The hardest thing for me is to stop thinking about issues I take home from work each day. It doesn't matter where I am or what I'm doing . . . there's always some unsolved problem from work that interrupts my thoughts.

I have trouble saying no when people ask me to do things. Even if I'm overburdened already, I still get hooked in when someone says, "Oh, you've *got* to do this for me."

I used to think when I reached this level of success I'd have it made. But now I find myself worrying about losing what I have and needing to achieve more just to prove I can still do it. I never thought I'd still be this driven, yet I'm pushing myself harder now than ever.

Who's Doing It to You?

Quite often we blame our workaholic tendencies on the company that employs us, the industry in which we work, or a particularly difficult boss. Yet if you examine closely what is driving you so hard, it usually has something to do with your work environment and a lot more to do with some emotional baggage from the past.

For example, Jerry is a sales representative who at the age of thirty-seven already has an ulcer, high blood pressure, and frequent backaches from his high pressure job. For many years, he thought the problem was because he worked in an extremely competitive field—selling financial investments.

So he switched industries and began selling computer software, but guess what happened? Once again he found himself working too hard and worrying too much. This time, however, he blamed it on his boss, whom he called a "neurotic noodge" (someone who tends to nag or give unsolicited advice and criticism).

Jerry quit that job, too, and decided to start his own company. Guess what happened this time? Even though he no longer had a boss to deal with, he and his business partner began driving each other crazy. Both of them competed over who was doing more and who was worth more to the company.

Finally, Jerry decided to buy out his partner and see if being completely on his own might make his work more enjoyable. Guess what happened this time? Like many self-employed people, Jerry was so afraid of failing that he began working even harder. His workaholic tendencies—which could no longer be blamed on a certain industry, boss or partner—now were even more threatening to Jerry's health and private life. Like the rest of us, Jerry had to look within for the reasons why he was pushing himself harder than necessary and making himself ill.

To help Jerry uncover some of the causes for his continual work tensions, I asked him to consider the following questions. See what comes to mind for you when you think about how these issues may be affecting your work life:

1. When you work too hard or worry too much, to whom are you being loyal? What person from your past (a parent, sibling, mentor, spouse, rival, or peer) are you trying to impress?

2. Now here's the ironic part. Does this person whom you're trying to impress know or care that you're making yourself ill in order to prove he or she was wrong about you?

3. When you work too hard or worry too much, for what event from the past are you trying to compensate? What are you afraid might happen again?

4. Have you forgiven yourself yet for not fulfilling all the expectations people put on you? Have you forgiven yourself yet for not fulfilling all the expectations you put on yourself?

When you think about these questions or discuss them with a supportive friend or counselor, you will probably gain valuable insights into what drives you so hard. Most people have set up a no-win situation for themselves. They are driving themselves crazy in order to make up for some past experience in which they felt they had let someone down. Or they are trying enormously hard to prove that the people who said "you aren't good enough" were wrong. Yet the effort doesn't reduce the inner turmoil. No matter how hard you try to prove yourself, the inner voice that says, "Sorry, you still have further to go," never lets up.

When Jerry set aside some uninterrupted time to examine what from his past might be propelling him to work too hard and worry too much, he found several valuable clues. According to Jerry, "Even though I'm finally self-employed, I realize that I'm still dancing to the tune set by other people. All my life there's been someone telling me I'm not quite good enough. At one time it was my parents, who thought I should be the best at everything I set out to do. Then it was my ex-wife, whom I wanted so badly to impress. Then it was my former boss, and later it was my business partner. I've tried so hard to please everyone and yet I'm still working my butt off hoping to convince myself they were wrong about me. When does it end? When do I get to feel pretty good inside and not trying to convince everyone I'm better than what I am?"

Like many of us who put more stress on ourselves than necessary, Jerry began noticing that "whenever things go wrong or I'm up against a deadline, I feel like it's a do-or-die situation in which my entire self-worth is on the line. I know intellectually that's not true—business associates who've been satisfied with my work for years are not going to lose all respect for me if I make one mistake. Yet in my gut, I'm still terrified a foul-up will permit those voices from my past to comment once again, 'See, we knew you couldn't do it. It was only a matter of time.' "

For Jerry to improve on his workaholic tendencies, he needed to stop being run by his insecurities from long ago. Gradually, over a twelve-month period, he began making progress, but it wasn't easy. Like most "reforming workaholics," Jerry discovered that whenever customers or associates made demands on him, he had to stop and catch himself from falling back into the pattern of overworking to please everybody.

He admits, "Learning to work effectively without overworking has been one of the most challenging things I've ever done. It was just as tough as quitting smoking or going on a diet. Yet the results are worth it. Regaining control over my work anxieties has freed up time and energy to begin a new relationship. My friends and my two children from my previous marriage say they can see the difference in me. Instead of a driven fool, I'm acting like a human being again."

The Reformed Workaholic's Bill of Rights

To break out of the trap of working too hard or worrying too much, you may have to give up a lot. You may need to stop trying to be all things to all people. You may have to give up your most familiar image of yourself as a frenetic, burdened and stressed out victim of your job. You may need to become the only nonworkaholic person in your department or company. It may even be necessary to let go of your deeply held belief that work is drudgery or, in the words of a T-shirt I saw recently, "Life is the pits and then you die." That belief by itself could be your biggest enemy.

Is regaining your sanity worth it? Surely you could follow the crowd and drive yourself to the point where you either dread each working day or find yourself saddled with premature stress-related illnesses. Or you might find your loved ones abandoning you because of how much your obsession with work has made them feel abandoned.

To help you see the challenge we all face to come to terms with our workaholic tendencies, consider the following. I call it the Bill of Rights for reformed workaholics:

1. *You have the right to say no to demands that you work harder than your creativity, health or family obligations can handle.*

If a boss, co-worker, or even yourself demands of you something that is unreasonable or is likely to be counterproductive in the long run because you know it will push you across the line into burnout, you have the right to say no. You owe it to your employer, your peers, and yourself not to say yes to something you can't do well because of competing demands on your time or energy. Quite often if you simply start turning down 10 percent of the unreasonable or excessive demands on you, the change in your health and outlook will be noticeable.

2. *You have the right to delegate the work you don't enjoy or don't have time and energy to do effectively.*

You are the only one who can decide the value of your time. If you are worth ten, fifty, or a hundred dollars an hour, you certainly can afford to pay someone else a lower amount to take a load of anxiety-producing excess work off your hands. By freeing your mind and restoring your creativity, you can achieve unexpected breakthroughs from good ideas that come to you during relaxing moments that would have been lost doing busy-work. Many of the most brilliant inventions, creative ideas, and problem-solving innovations have come to people not when they were stressed but when they took time to relax and unwind.

3. *You have the right to schedule rest, relaxation, and fun with as much assertiveness as you would schedule work-related appointments.*

If someone asked you to ignore your plans for an important business appointment, you'd tell them, "Sorry, I've made plans I can't change. We'll have to get together some other time." Yet if something came up to upset your plans for a relaxing lunch, an hour of uninterrupted exercise, an evening of enjoying family, friends, or a good book, you probably would abandon those needs in an instant. Why are we so firm in holding to our work commitments and so easily sidetracked when it comes to taking care of our health or enjoying our time off? Since workaholics know how to keep their commitments, you should start taking your commitments to yourself and your need for relaxation and fun more seriously. Just as you wouldn't cancel a business appointment for the wrong reasons, so should you avoid canceling breaks, exercise, and vacations.

4. *You have the right to listen to your body when it tells you it's time to slow down.*

Each of us has powerful early warning signals that tell us when it's time to reduce our stress levels or else risk burnout, inefficiency, and possible illness. What are your earliest clues that you're working too hard and starting to lose your clarity? It might be a cold or flu, a skin flare-up, a stomach, back, or head pain. It might be when you notice your patience is short or you are snapping at loved ones. It pays to know yourself and to appreciate your limits if you are to enjoy your work.

5. *You have the right to schedule a cushion each day to prevent burnout.*

If you make sure you've added at least an hour each day for delays and unexpected interruptions, you won't feel so harried and angry when things go wrong. If you set aside time for a short rest, a relaxing walk, or opportunities to browse and brainstorm each day, you will be surprised at how creative and productive you can be. Build into your schedule enough time to deal with the emotional concerns that come up regularly. Instead of stuffing your feelings inside because there's no time to air your concerns, be certain you resolve misunderstandings and personality clashes as soon as possible. Otherwise you will carry them around as emotional baggage with far more destructive effects than if you take the time to work things out soon after they occur.

6. *You have the right to feel successful and worthwhile even if your work or your income doesn't fit the pictures you grew up with.*

Quite often the interesting and important work we do in life is not what we intended or what our backgrounds prepared us to do. You may need to let go of your earlier pictures of success and fulfillment to appreciate fully the accomplishments and progress you are making. If you were your own best therapist, what would you see as the successes and strengths of this person called you? What unrealistic standards of perfection would you want your patient to eliminate? What special talents and skills would you want to encourage?

7. *You have the right to celebrate even the smallest successes.*

Most people are great at noticing mistakes or things that haven't been completed yet. On the other hand, they are reluctant to admit things that are going well for fear it will mysteriously cause them to disappear.

The best way to start enjoying your work life is to make sure you notice every day your smallest successes. When you stop and acknowledge yourself for how well you handled a particular challenge, it gives you energy to carry on. When you take note of how much progress you are making in areas that used to overwhelm you, it gives you courage to face your next challenge.

One way to break the habit of working too hard with no sense of satisfaction is to use a simple exercise that can be done alone or with a partner every night. Either on a sheet of paper or out loud, list "Three things that went well today . . ." If you do this with a partner, you will find that instead of feeling sluggish and alienated from each other every night, you will feel energized and more intimate.

Your work life occupies a major percentage of your time on Earth. Whether it will feel like a burden or a source of satisfaction is up to you. Now is the time to unravel why you're stuck in a rut or not feeling good about how you spend so much of your energy.

Part Three:
Finding Support to Make
Your Success Less Stressful

Once upon a time, success was an easy concept to understand. For some it meant having a good job, a good income, a house, two cars, a dog, and a big insurance policy. For others it meant running a good household, having a good relationship, and raising healthy children.

These days it's much harder to know if you are successful or not, especially since so many people are trying to be successful in several areas at once—career and money-making, family and relationships, personal growth and inner peace. Very few of us were raised to take on all these challenges at the same time. Hardly any of us have healthy role models that tell us how to balance the conflicting demands of work, family, a love life, and an inner life.

Since each of us is essentially a trailblazer in this new era of changing sex roles, changing work values, and changing lifestyles, we have two choices about how we will navigate our way through the obstacles and challenges. One method is to try to do it all alone, avoiding the advice or support that others who have walked a similar path might give us. The other method is to find creative ways to get support and share experiences with people who understand the challenges we have taken on.

Too often we don't feel successful in our lives because our daily accomplishments don't seem to fit the pictures we were raised with about success. For example, here are several admissions I've heard from women and men in group counseling sessions having to do with success and personal values:

> My problem is I work hard at my career but I still can't afford many of the things I thought I'd be able to afford when I reached this level of success. That makes me question whether or not I'm a failure.

> My trouble with work is that I want it to be easy. If it doesn't happen quickly I don't have the patience. So I've chased after several get-rich-quick schemes and never taken the time to build something gradually, step by step.

> My struggle has been trying to juggle too many things at once. Just when I've got my career under control, I

feel like a failure in my love life or with my kids. No matter how well I'm doing in one area of my life the turmoil in another area seems to carry over.

My fear is that only the driven and compulsive ones succeed in their fields. I've got other things to worry about—an aging parent, three teenage children, a spouse, and my friendships. Yet I still have goals and ambitions. I don't want to be left behind just because I can't devote twenty-four hours a day to my work.

In order to sort out the realistic and unnecessary worries each of us faces in our struggle to balance career and other priorities, it helps to have people you can talk to who understand what you're going through. Rather than confronting these complex issues all alone, it's more productive and enjoyable to get support and good ideas from creative minds who share your concerns. For example, here is a case that illustrates the benefits of seeking out special people who can assist you in making your current challenges less stressful:

"I Thought No One Else Could Understand"

Laureen is a divorced mother working to support two young children. Attempting to be a reliable breadwinner, a caring parent, and starting a new life of her own following her divorce had begun to take its toll. As she describes, "I felt like I was being punished for some reason. Why should anyone be asked to succeed at so many contradictory challenges all at once?"

Like many of us, Laureen's background had not prepared her for the many hats she now has to wear. According to her, "The only example I had about how to be successful in the world was my father who worked long hours, never got what he deserved, didn't want to discuss it or do anything to change his situation. On the other hand, there was my mother who would scream if she knew I was raising two children without a father or that I was trying to run my own business out of my living room."

Part of Laureen's problem was feeling alone and without any support in her struggle to balance so many difficult tasks. She admits, "For a long time I thought I was the only one going through this much turmoil. I didn't want to burden my friends by complaining or sounding like a victim. I assumed I was paying the price of having failed at marriage and that no one else could help."

As in so many cases, Laureen's breakthrough came once she found support and guidance from people who shared similar situations. One day in a bookstore, Laureen was browsing through a paperback called *Entrepreneurial Mothers*. In the back of the book, she found an address for an organization of home-based business owners. Soon she joined a support group of women like herself who shared concerns and offered helpful advice on everything from taxes and time-management to child care and resources for women entrepreneurs.

Laureen discovered that "several problems I thought no one could understand were things other women like myself were dealing with on a daily basis: How do you teach your kids whether to interrupt Mommy when she's working? How do you find quality people to handle the things you don't have time to do yourself? How do you find quiet time away from the kids and the business? How do you deal with the special problems of a shaky start-up operation during its first two years?"

Instead of blaming herself or feeling guilty for having to deal with such complex issues, Laureen discovered that "by putting our heads together, my support group gives me a host of alternatives for solving even the most difficult issues. Usually we don't even have to meet. One phone call to someone who knows what I'm going through can relieve those feelings of panic and give me several options that I might not have considered on my own."

As Laureen's case demonstrates, we each need creative and encouraging people who understand our particular work challenges. If the support group that addresses your specific career and personal issues doesn't already exist, then it's up to you to form one. Even if it's simply an informal group of three or more intelligent people you can call in the middle of a crisis to get understanding and good ideas, that could make the difference between feeling overwhelmed or enjoying your work.

Support groups can be as specific as "Asian-American Men in the Helping Professions" or "Divorced Mothers Reentering the Job Market." Support groups can also be as general as "Women in Management" or "Men in the Arts." What's important is that you don't need to feel alone or without creative options when your work becomes stressful or dissatisfying. Once you establish a network of several people who can appreciate your emotional concerns, help solve your business issues, and encourage your personal risks, you will quickly get back on track. Your work will feel more rewarding and less like a burden when you don't have to carry all the weight on your solitary shoulders.

Support groups can be beneficial especially during times when you are out of work or considering a job change. Not only do groups of well-connected individuals provide valuable contacts and job opportunities, but they help you feel included even when you are no longer a part of the same organization you worked with for years before quitting or losing your job. In addition, having a support group to suggest job-search strategies and encourage you after each rejection or delay can be a welcome contrast to impersonal classified ads and cold calls to prospective employers.

Too many people feel guilty or inadequate for having

work-related concerns that don't disappear overnight. You must recognize that, especially in these complex times, the challenge of balancing career demands with your other priorities is a very formidable task. Instead of keeping your concerns silent or trying to solve them all alone, now might be a good time to share your experiences and questions with others. Even if you feel your background hasn't prepared you for the many hats you currently wear, it's never too soon to start resolving the tensions that are affecting your life. As Anna Freud once said, "Creative minds have been known to overcome any kind of bad training." By finding support from others who are on a similiar path, your challenges may become less stressful.

Repairing Strained Relations with Difficult Family Members

5

> We can hardly deal with such grand issues as world peace until we make peace with those closest to us.
>
> —Marilyn Ferguson

If you ask most people whether they love the members of their immediate family, they usually will say, "Yes, of course." However, if you ask them whether they *like* each of their immediate family members, that's a tougher question.

Whether we admit it or not, nearly every one of us has at least one close relative or family member with whom we don't get along. It might be a parent or child from whom you have grown emotionally distant. It could be a brother or sister who frequently gets on your nerves. It might be an in-law, stepparent or other relative who is in your life to stay but for whom you have little warmth or even tolerance.

To be honest, if you weren't related to this person you probably wouldn't be friends or see each other as often as you do now. In many cases, the only reason you are civil to this individual is to prevent additional hurt feelings or nasty encounters.

In your own family situation, who are the individuals that give you the most trouble? Who is the relative you would least like to spend time with on a desert island?

Who is the person that always manages to make you or a loved one feel unwelcome at family events? Who is the family member that brings out the worst in you?

The Costs of Ignoring Your Family Tensions

Even the mention of this family member may cause you to ask, "Do I really have to deal with this?"

As a young child, you probably were forced to be nice to all your relatives even if they weren't nice to you. You probably were instructed not to admit out loud that there were battles in your family or that you couldn't stand someone's treatment of you.

However, now that you're an adult it's not because of family pride or to please other people that you need to work through your tensions with difficult family members. The person who is hurting the most from the unresolved conflict is you. The person who has the most to gain by working through the tensions is you.

Some of the costs you might be paying for having a strained relationship with a member of your family are:

—Feeling angry or upset after a phone call with this person. The tension from the phone call frequently gets taken out on your loved ones, co-workers, or on your own health and well-being.

—Dreading family get-togethers. Instead of enjoying the rare times your blood relatives get together for holidays, birthdays, and other "celebrations," you may find yourself bending over backward to please the very same person you don't like. You may be so afraid of a blow-up that you spend the entire get-together being polite.

—Feeling guilty and incomplete when a close relative, parent, child, or sibling is ill or dying. Too often we wait until it's too late to work through our differences with a loved one and then regret missing out on the closeness that could have been.

—Failing to give your own children a sense of extended family because of your unfinished business with certain relatives. Even though your children enjoy the attentions of grandparents, aunts, uncles, and other relatives, you might be restricting their family contacts because of your own conflicts with those individuals.

—Overreacting to anyone who reminds you of the family member you detest. When a spouse, lover, friend, or co-worker does anything that resembles the relative who gets on your nerves, you may unknowingly dump a load of resentments on that undeserving person.

—Carrying more than your share of bitterness and alienation because of your unresolved tensions with your family. Even though you might think it's no big deal to be in conflict with a family member, it could be weighing you down emotionally and adding unnecessary tensions and worries to your everyday life.

Stubbornness on Both Sides

Despite the costs of maintaining a strained relationship with a family member, most people try to pretend the problem doesn't exist rather than working through their feelings. For example, Gordon is a successful business executive who hasn't spoken to his grown-up son Andy for almost five years. To outsiders, Gordon insists he's not bothered by the lack of communication between him and his only son. While he says, "That's just the way things are sometimes. I've gotten used to it," his wife Julianne tells a different story.

According to her, "The ongoing battle between Gordon and Andy is slowly eating away at each of us. When I talk to Andy, I can hear in his voice how much he loves his Dad but he doesn't want to make the first move. When I talk to Gordon, I hear him defending why he refuses to call Andy but I also hear his pain.

"Last month we attended a wedding in which our best friends' son got married. It was a gorgeous day, and the wedding was especially beautiful. But what I remember the most is sitting next to Gordon and watching the tears stream down his face. Those weren't tears of joy for the groom and his parents. Those tears were because he misses Andy and yet he still won't reach out. I wish these two stubborn men would realize what everyone else sees is so obvious—they love each other and neither one will be happy until they work through their differences."

Long-Distance Tensions

When you or I carry unresolved bitterness toward a close family member, every phone call or visit is one more chance for the resentments to surface. No amount of time or geographical distance can protect you from the necessity of cleaning up unfinished business with a family member who, for better or worse, plays an important role in your life.

As an example, Margaret is a forty-year-old television producer who lives more than three thousand miles from the rest of her family. Yet the unresolved feelings she has toward certain family members are just as strong as if she saw them on a daily basis.

Recently Margaret's momentous fortieth-birthday party was going fine until she received a long-distance phone call from her younger sister Karen. Besides wishing Margaret a happy birthday, she passed along a piece of news that put a damper on the celebration—Karen had called to announce she was pregnant.

While Margaret pretended to be happy for her sister, in fact the announcement brought up painful feelings about Margaret's own desire to have children. Only three years earlier she was engaged, but the marriage was called off. At the time, she confided in her younger sister Karen. Yet instead of support and comfort, Karen gave Margaret an insensitive response, reminding Margaret she never was very good at relationships.

The news about Karen's pregnancy also brought up memories of another painful episode between the two sisters. When Margaret was in college, she spent several weeks agonizing over a difficult decision whether to terminate an unwanted pregnancy she had with a man who was reluctant to get married. At the time, Margaret had begged Karen not to tell their mother about the abortion, but Karen had informed her anyway.

After getting off the phone with Karen, Margaret felt a rush of intense anger and resentment. This was not the first time a long-distance phone call from her sister or mother had ruined a happy moment in her life. Even though Margaret had been feeling forty years young before Karen's call, the stirring up of old wounds with her younger sister made Margaret feel a lot older and not in the mood for celebrating.

What Can Be Done?

If you have had enough of your battles with a certain relative, now is the right time to try something new. If you are ready to let go of your bitterness, and instead find a way to regain the sense of connection and love you once had with this person, there are several options that have proven successful for thousands of women and men whose family members were at least as difficult as yours.

Before you set out to improve the relationship, however, you must become aware of several strategies that don't work. Too often people with good intentions for resolving a family conflict make the following kinds of mistakes.

I call these "The Guaranteed Ways to Make a Family Conflict Even Worse." See how many of them you have tried in the past:

—*Wearing a forced smile in the hope your family member won't guess how angry you are.* Have you ever sat through a holiday dinner or other family gathering with a frozen smile on your face, as if to say, "Hey, don't worry about me. I'm just fine." Meanwhile you feel like screaming and your face begins to hurt from holding that smile too long. In addition, your head aches and your stomach churns from the resentments you've stuffed inside. Yet you still want everyone to think you're having the time of your life.

—*Trying to reform your relatives.* Some people give lots of advice to a difficult family member, hoping that out of respect for you this person will magically change an irritating habit he or she has possessed for a lifetime. If you are waiting for your family members to change miraculously and finally live up to your expectations, my only advice would be, "You should live so long."

—*Stuffing your face with food to keep your mind off the family tensions.* Most people arrive at a family dinner promising themselves, "This time I won't overeat. Even if they insist, I'll say no to that second helping and that third piece of dessert." Yet as soon as the arguments, criticisms, and power struggles begin again, you notice yourself stuffing your face in order to stay out of the conflict. For days afterward you feel bloated and angry for overeating at another family event. Why is it that instead of resolving our differences with family members we swallow our pride along with a quantity of food we would never consume at any other type of social gathering?

—*Waiting for a provocation so you can blame your adversary.* Sometimes we show up at a family gathering with the attitude, "If so-and-so mentions one more word about _____, I'm going to explode." Invariably, so-and-so *will* utter the words that set you off and once again the hostilities will escalate. Looking for an excuse so you can act self-righteous and wronged is one of the surest ways to make a family conflict even worse.

—*Making sacrifices in the hope your relative will feel guilty and give in.* How often have you pretended to be forgiving and generous when in fact you were still seething inside? How many times have you made compromises or sacrifices that were not reciprocated by the other person? The dispute with a close relative will not be over simply because one or both sides acts like a martyr and pretends the conflict is resolved. It will take one or both of you honestly working through your tensions and no longer feeling like a victim before the cycle of accusations and resentments is broken.

—*Refusing to budge until the other person apologizes first.* This strategy is the flip side of the one described above. Too often we expect the other person to take all the blame or make sacrifices on our behalf before we will trust them again. While it would be great if every person who got on your nerves immediately apologized, this doesn't happen too often. My only advice on waiting for others to apologize first is, "Don't hold your breath."

—*Rationalizing that the tension between you and this close relative isn't hurting.* This clever bit of dishonesty is the most frequent mistake people make that allows family conflicts to fester and grow. All you have to do is add up the number of hours you've spent feeling angry or deliberating what to do about this person and you will see the conflict is costing you more than you can afford. The tensions will not disappear if you push them under the carpet or rationalize that this person isn't worth getting upset about. Face it—you're not happy with the situation and it's time to take constructive steps to improve it. The longer you put it off, the more inflexible and bitter both sides will become.

Taking Charge of the Situation

Most people feel powerless to do anything about a conflict they're having with a family member. I often hear remarks like:

I've tried everything but this person is impossible.

I think he (or she) does this just to see how much it will upset me.

No one gets along with this person. Why should I be different?

It's been this way as long as I can remember. There's no reason to think it's going to get better.

I give up. I just can't put any more effort into an impossible situation.

If you tend to feel there's nothing left that might improve your strained relationship with a difficult family member (or anyone else who's in your life to stay), I urge you to look again at the situation. There may be steps you can take that avoid the pitfalls you've encountered in the past. There may be strategies you can use that don't set yourself up for defeat or discouragement. You might be able to feel resolved and at peace about this difficult person even if he or she doesn't budge an inch. Here's how it has been done successfully by people I've counseled in the past:

Part One:
Improvements You Can Make Without the
Other Person's Cooperation

1. *Find out why you've let the other person control the relationship.* Even if you have spent years letting the other person dictate how the relationship will be, it's not too late to try something new. Part of discovering your own power in the situation is recognizing how and why you've surrendered your power in the past. For example, here are several insights people have uncovered about why they feel powerless to deal with a difficult family member. See how many ring true in your family conflict:

I feel powerless compared to _____ because I've always been younger. Even though I'm an adult now, I still relate to _____ as if I were a child.

I think _____ and I got off on the wrong foot. When we first met and realized we were going to be part of the same family, it was a very hectic time for both of us. I think we each were at our worst then and we've never worked through what happened in those early days.

I don't get along with _____ because the relationship is so one-sided. My _____ makes demands and I either go along or rebel. If it's ever going to improve, I've got to find a way to say no sometimes and to ask for what I need. It can't remain this one-sided.

In my family, any disagreement or dissent is heresy. Years ago I tried to change a few things, but the flack I got wasn't worth it. Now I just keep my mouth shut, especially since my _____ has been ill. I don't want to make any waves in case she gets worse or if she dies.

My problem is that I act as if my family conflicts don't get to me. I can joke about them, but deep inside there's a lot of pain I don't acknowledge. As I get older I'm starting to worry that I'll always be the distant observer with my relatives. I'm afraid I'll never really connect with them again.

In each of the above statements, notice how hard it is for us to change a family relationship that started out badly or that has been in a rut for years. In some cases, we continue to feel younger and less powerful than our older family members. In other cases, an incident or bad experience from long ago still clouds our thoughts. Finally, there are situations in which the family is structured so that certain people (such as the eldest, the males, the loudest, the richest, or the most hysterical) tend to win while the others are treated like doormats.

To improve an uneven relationship isn't easy but it can be done. It must begin, however, with your knowing exactly what *you* do to perpetuate the problem. Do you act more immature with this particular relative than with anyone else in your life? Do you hold back your opinions, feelings, and needs? Do you give in when it might be a better idea to be assertive? Do you allow this person to treat you badly in ways you wouldn't allow anyone else? Certainly the other person plays an important role in the relationship, yet if you uncover your own contribution to the problem, at least then you will be able to change your half of the uneven relationship. When you stop acting in a way that allows this person to dominate you, he or she will have to adjust to your new ways.

2. *Rather than taking your resentments out on this person, find a way to work through your anger and hurt on your own or with a supportive friend or counselor.* The best place to begin repairing a strained family relationship is by reducing the emotional load you've been carry-

ing with regard to the conflict. For example, if you work through your resentments and anger immediately after a difficult phone call or visit, you can avoid carrying it into your daily life and your next phone call or visit.

Sheila's story illustrates well the importance of working out your anger as soon as possible. A home-based business woman, Sheila used to feel upset or depressed the entire day after a morning phone call from her difficult mother-in-law. According to Sheila, "After a call from her, I couldn't concentrate on my work for hours. Calling back only made things worse."

Now Sheila has three different techniques that work successfully whenever an invasive or critical phone call from her mother-in-law, her mother, or a difficult business associate gets on her nerves. Sometimes Sheila pounds a mattress with her fists for ten minutes until the resentments subside. Other times she regains her concentration and motivation to work by drawing several angry sketches of the interaction with her difficult relative. If neither of those techniques do the trick, she takes twenty minutes off to relax, unwind, and write an angry letter that she doesn't send but which gets the resentments out of her system quickly and safely. Here is an example of one of Sheila's unmailed letters. She wrote it after her mother-in-law spent nearly a half hour telling Sheila about her aches and pains.

Dear Gloria (Sheila's mother-in-law),

I just got off the phone with you and I feel like screaming. You spent the whole time complaining about your problems and once again refused to listen to any advice, refused to go to see a doctor, and interrupted me every time I tried to speak.

I hate when you do that. I am *not* your toxic waste dump that you can call me up whenever you want and complain to your heart's content with no opportunity for me to respond. I don't know where you learned such disrespect for other people but it's not going to continue.

Next time you want to complain and not let me respond, I'm going to interrupt you just like you interrupt me. And if you won't go to a doctor or take care of yourself, I'm going to tell you, Gloria, that it's about time you grew up and stopped acting like a helpless child.

I've got the answering machine on now and believe me, I'm not going to pick it up unless it's someone I want to talk to. Someone who not only talks but listens. And if you want to have a conversation with me where both of us respect each other, great! If not, you can talk to your son. I love you a lot, which doesn't mean I have to be your dumping ground.

Even though Sheila would never say these things to her mother-in-law in person, she realizes that by writing them down—in an angry letter which she doesn't send—something remarkable occurs. The tensions and frustrations from the phone call become less oppressive. Within minutes, Sheila feels productive and focused again on her work. Instead of spending the day arguing in her mind with her mother-in-law, she spends it getting things done and feeling resolved about the situation. Sheila's example shows how releasing anger quickly on your own can be a safe and effective method to keep a difficult relative from ruining your day.

3. *You can prepare ahead of time for a challenging call or visit.* Another benefit of letting go of resentments is that it increases the likelihood of a healthier interaction next time. When you work through your anger, guilt, and distrust ahead of time, you won't be as easily thrown off center by anything your difficult family member does or says. Even if the person continues to do what used to

drive you crazy, now that you've worked through your resentments on your own, her or his actions will have much less negative effect on you.

For example, an excellent technique to prepare ahead of time for a challenging family visit or phone call is the "Guilt-Desensitization Exercise" Dr. Harold Bloomfield and I describe in our book *Making Peace With Your Parents*. It can help you defuse the most typical lines your relative tends to hit you with that drive you crazy. For instance, what in your family are the lines that make you want to scream? In most families, they sound like, "Are you eating right?," "Did you forget to send _____ a birthday card?," "When are you getting married?," "Why don't you call more often?," etc.

The Guilt-Desensitization Exercise allows you to practice hearing statements like these and, instead of feeling guilty or victimized, seeing the repetitiveness and humor contained in the lines. Briefly summarized, the instructions are as follows:

1. In a voice that resembles your difficult family member, talk into a tape recorder or have a friend practice saying the five most nagging things you tend to hear during a family visit or phone call.

2. While relaxing, breathing slowly in and out, and listening for humor, play back your tape of the five best lines (or have your friend recite them back to you).

3. Notice your breathing and make sure you keep relaxing, inhaling and exhaling slowly, and listening for the humor. Appreciate just how absurd it is that you are being asked for the 789th time, "You don't want more to eat? What's the matter—don't you like my cooking?"

4. Then, when you are talking with your difficult family member, remember to breathe in and out slowly,

relax, and appreciate the humor that he or she is doing the very same things you predicted.

Here's an illustration of how the Guilt-Desensitization Exercise works:

When Ted, a struggling writer, used to visit or talk with his older brother Victor, a successful businessman, Ted would seethe with anger and feel trapped by Victor's repetitive questions and condescending attitude. According to Ted, "Even if I'd had a good week recently, after ten minutes with Victor I'd end up feeling inadequate, defensive and guilty. Victor is an M.B.A. with as much sensitivity and warmth as an automated teller machine. Since he's always been my elder, he knows exactly what to say to make me feel small."

To prepare for his next close encounter of the family kind, Ted did the Guilt-Desensitization Exercise and tape recorded the following five typical lines he often hears from Victor:

When are you going to grow up and stop being such a dreamer?

Why don't you call the folks more often and stop being so selfish?

When are you getting married?

Why can't you practice religion the way the rest of us do?

When are you going to start saving for the future?

After practicing several times how to relax and remain centered even when hearing those lines coming from the tape recorder, Ted was ready for his next conversation with Victor. At a birthday celebration a few weeks later, Ted found himself alone with Victor. Normally that would have put a damper on the entire evening. This time, however, when Victor started into his usual barrage of questions, Ted was ready. Relaxing and remaining calm, Ted heard Victor start talking about, "When are you going to stop being such a dreamer?" Instead of feeling belittled, Ted smiled from the familiarity of his older brother's repetitiveness. Saying to himself, "Hey, there it is—good old number one from the exercise," Ted was able for the very first time to dodge his brother's verbal assaults without taking on a load of undeserved criticism.

This Guilt-Desensitization Exercise can help you turn a family get-together or phone call from an anxious burden into a more relaxed event. Simply by taking the sting out of the repetitive themes and criticisms heaped on you by difficult family members, you have a better chance to retain your peace of mind and not become overwhelmed or shut down by an insensitive remark. Instead of feeling depressed for days afterward, you can laugh at the absurdity of how frequently your difficult family member dwells on the same issues.

4. *You can work toward forgiving this person for incidents that happened long ago.* Another significant step you can take without the other person's cooperation is to decide when and if you are ready to forgive. A family member may have betrayed your trust or treated you badly some time ago. As a result, you have been carrying a grudge that gets heavier with each passing year. Now might be a good opportunity to reexamine the situation, work through your hurt, and take the next step to lighten your load of resentment.

One warning, however, about forgiveness. Too often I have seen people with legitimate anger and still unresolved hurts get talked into forgiving someone before this person is ready to forgive. Some therapists, workshop leaders, clergy, or friends might make it sound as though you can simply snap your fingers and say, "I forgive this person who did this terrible thing to me." Yet in your heart you still feel injured from the long-ago incident and unresolved about the reasons why this awful experience occurred in the first place. The smile on your face may signify forgiveness, yet the churning in your stomach tells you there's still unfinished business to resolve.

Most of us want to forgive, yet forgiveness entails a lot more than simply snapping our fingers and saying, "Poof, it's gone." In fact, you may have said in the past that you have forgiven someone in your family, yet your anger and hurt tell you there's still more work to be done.

I advise a different approach. While I agree that forgiveness is a powerful healing device both for the person you forgive and also for yourself, I believe it's self-defeating to forgive before you're ready. I advise you to take a few preliminary steps to clear out the emotional baggage that might prevent you from truly forgiving someone, especially a close family member who did something terrible to you. Only when you work through these unresolved concerns will your forgiveness be genuine and long-lasting.

The steps I recommend if you want to forgive with integrity are:

—Research the reasons why this person was driven to do the awful thing that hurt you. Talk to other relatives who can provide background information about why this family member acted the way he or she did. Quite often you will find your difficult family member had painful experiences in his or her background that partially explain why this person mistreated you. *That doesn't excuse the actions but it gives you some insight into the behavior.*

—Look at the situation from the other person's point of view. What did she or he think was happening at the time, even if this perception was faulty or insensitive? What did your family member believe might be gained by treating you in such an unfeeling way? What hurt from the past was this person trying to resolve? What loss or emptiness was this person seeking to overcome? Once again, this doesn't excuse what was done to you. It merely allows you the perspective to make a free decision—do you want to forgive this person or not?

—What has been done, or what can be done, to remedy what this person did? Quite often the key to forgiveness is not that everyone should smile and say things are peachy, but rather that the person who hurt you has begun to change or grow from learning the lessons of his or her insensitive behavior. In most cases, you shouldn't expect to change this person all by yourself. Your best option is to make sure this person seeks expert help to resolve the habit that was taken out on you.

—Finally, think about the benefits available to you if you forgive this person and stop holding the grudge that has been taking up so much emotional energy all these years. Forgiving him or her doesn't mean what was done isn't wrong and not to be tolerated in the future. It doesn't mean you should whitewash the situation or once again put blind trust in someone who's likely to abuse your trust.

Forgiveness simply means you're ready to let go and move on. In the words of Gandhi, forgiveness requires only that you "Hate the sin but love the sinner." To forgive is defined as a release from resentment, an end to your need for revenge or payment. It means you can get on with your life. It is for your own emotional healing more than it is for the other person's guilt or innocence.

Vicki's case is a good illustration of the importance of forgiving a close family member despite the insensitivity of what that person did. When Vicki was in college, she fell in love with and wanted to marry a man who came from a different religious and ethnic background. To Vicki's surprise, her parents and older siblings reacted much worse than expected.

According to Vicki, "I knew they might not like my marrying outside the religion, but I had no idea the depth of feeling or the rude behavior it would provoke. My family treated my boyfriend as though he were a criminal and even threatened to disown me. When I refused to give in to their demands, they became even more desperate. My father refused to come to our wedding, so instead my boyfriend and I eloped."

For years, Vicki has remained distant and resentful with her family. Yet in the past few months, something happened to change that situation. Her aging father has been hospitalized with a stroke and the doctors aren't sure how long he'll be alive. For the first time since college, Vicki is thinking about reestablishing some closeness with her family, yet her anger about the way they treated her boyfriend still feels like an insurmountable obstacle.

When I suggested that Vicki use the steps described above to research her family's point of view about the marriage controversy, she was at first reluctant. "Why should I consider their feelings when they've never considered mine," she asked.

I reminded her that the reason to understand and forgive our family members is not to be nice or to whitewash what others have done. I described how "the benefits are for you. This may be your last opportunity to connect with your father and let go of the hurts that have kept you separate for so long. You're not doing it to excuse your family's intolerance but to regain an important bond with these people you've never stopped loving."

Over a period of several weeks, Vicki set out to understand more fully the reasons why her family had reacted with such anger and rudeness many years ago. Like any research project, finding out why your family members did something that hurt you will take persistence and creativity. Vicki talked to aunts, uncles, cousins, an old college teacher of hers, and read several books on the subjects of intermarriage and religious identity. The more she understood about the personal and cultural reasons why her family had been so intolerant, the easier it was for her to work through her resentments.

As Vicki explains, "Even though I still don't like the way my relatives acted, I understand it differently now. Learning more about how my parents were raised and why they feel so inflexible on this issue, I can appreciate their reasons without necessarily having to agree with them. Despite what happened and the hurt they caused, I've finally found it in my heart to forgive them. My father and the other family members aren't perfect by any means, yet they're still my family. I can't help loving them and wanting to connect despite our differences."

Vicki's case illustrates why letting go of resentments and resolving issues from the past is so important. Underneath the anger and hurt we feel toward a difficult family member, we still have a deep desire to love and be loved by those closest to us. No matter how far we separate ourselves geographically or emotionally from our family members, our unfinished business is carried with us.

Part Two:
Improvements You Can Make
Involving the Other Person

Only when you have completed one or more of the above steps on your own are you ready for the next challenge—what to do when you actually see your difficult relative again. Here are some guidelines to help you avoid falling into the same habits and conflicts with this person:

1. *Try something new and experiment with different ways of spending time together.* Most family members see each other only in large group events (dinners, weddings, religious holidays, birthdays, funerals, etc.). When too many egos are gathered together, it's next to impossible to have a relaxed and satisfying conversation with any family member, especially the one with whom you've been having trouble.

For example, have you ever noticed how at large family gatherings, the odds of getting interrupted each time you speak are much higher than at other times? Too often a few overbearing relatives dominate the discussions while the rest sit back and pray it will be over soon. In addition, most family get-togethers center around more food, liquor, and television than usual. How are you going to connect with this difficult relative when everyone is shouting, "Eat! Eat!" or "Shhhh! We can't hear the television program while you're talking."

You shouldn't depend on large family events as your only chance to resolve your tensions with this particular relative. Why not try a more relaxed and enjoyable setting for getting to know this person in a new light? How about doing something that is closer to both of your interests—attend a concert, go to an amusement park, have lunch at your favorite restaurant, enjoy a sporting event, spend a day at a health spa together, or prepare a relaxing picnic and take a walk in the park. You both will feel more like yourselves in small, intimate settings. Use your imagination to come up with several options you and this person haven't tried for a long while.

The variety of ways to connect in a more relaxed fashion with this difficult family member are limitless. Here are several examples I've seen that might stimulate some ideas for your situation.

—Two sisters who had grown apart because of differing lifestyles became friends again when they started to go to museums together a few times a year.

—Two brothers who thought they had nothing in common began to talk openly with each other again during a weekend camping trip that renewed their closeness.

—A mother and daughter, who thought the only way they could be together was to argue, discovered by attending a night school class together that they once again enjoyed each other's company.

—A father and son who could never find time for each other began to build a friendship by getting together for a long lunch once a week.

What's it going to take for you and your difficult family member to break out of your rut and finally enjoy the time you spend together? The answer lies in your creativity and persistence—don't give up if your first few attempts to be with one another turn out to be dreadful. Eventually you may find there's a way to enjoy being together despite your differences.

2. *Be realistic about the length and frequency of phone calls and visits.* Even if your family tradition is that you have to talk to certain relatives every day of the week, maybe it's time to break the tradition, especially if you and this person have traditionally gotten on each other's nerves. Or if the family habit is long, difficult visits with out-of-town relatives, maybe it's time to break that habit and initiate something that is more enjoyable for everyone involved.

Getting along better with a difficult family member *doesn't* mean you have to become roommates or best friends. It doesn't obligate you to put up with invasive and overlong phone calls. Nor does it require you to visit more often or for longer amounts of time than is comfortable for you.

For example, Joan hasn't been getting along well with her grown-up daughter for several years. Yet out of tradition, she visits her daughter for a month every summer or winter. When I asked Joan how long it takes for her and her daughter to get on each other's nerves, she knew without stopping to think it takes about four days. According to Joan, "We do fine the first day or two catching up on each other's lives. Then we usually enjoy some activity my daughter has planned. But after four or five days, we start to criticize and feel claustrophobic spending so much time together."

Would Joan consider shortening her yearly visits from a month to a week? Joan looked shocked when I suggested it.

"My daughter would think I don't love her if I said I was only coming for seven days," she replied. "Besides, it's so expensive."

Yet when Joan tried my suggestion, she found that this one-week visit was her most pleasurable ever. She describes, "We were glad to see each other and we didn't grow tired of one another as we usually do. After seven days, I went and stayed with some other old friends from years ago and did some sightseeing. Instead of feeling drained and upset with my daughter for the umpteenth time, this visit left me feeling energized and looking forward to our next get-together, which we've decided should be sooner than our customary once-a-year."

The improvement experienced by Joan and her daughter is similar to those achieved by many others who took the initiative to break family tradition and experiment with different lengths and logistics for visits with relatives. The sooner you let go of rigid habits and rules that don't work for the parties involved, the sooner you can begin asking yourself and each other, "What is the best way for us to connect that doesn't turn into a burden or an unfulfilling obligation?"

The same principle of choosing what works over what is habitual applies to phone calls as well. Trish and her older sister Beth used to call each other nearly every day out of habit. According to Trish, "Even if we had very little to say to one another, we'd spend a lot of time on the phone. Invariably, we'd be giving each other unsolicited advice and criticism. Or we'd bring each other down because when you talk to someone that often, you can't help getting impatient with the way they're handling their life."

When Trish first suggested that she and Beth should talk only once a week, Beth's reaction was surprise, as she admits, "I thought it meant Trish was mad at me about something. Then I found out it wasn't out of anger or disrespect that Trish wanted to talk less often. She suggested and I eventually agreed that if we had one good conversation every week or so it was going to make us closer than if we struggled to find things to talk about more often than that."

According to Trish, "That one small change in our relationship—calling less frequently—has done a lot for both of us. I'm much more understanding and affectionate now that I know I'm not talking to her every day. She's more like an old friend now that I *want* to talk to, rather than a family member I *have* to talk to."

3. *Remember to keep yourself healthy, both physically and emotionally, during a family visit.* Many people who diligently exercise, stretch, relax, and avoid certain harmful foods most of the time somehow neglect all their good habits when they are visiting relatives. After a short amount of time, they feel stressed and anxious, blaming it all on their difficult relatives. Yet it's up to each of us to remain healthy and relaxed even when we are with our families.

Before your next get-together, make sure you set aside time to put yourself in the best frame of mind for the visit. Spend a few hours prior to the family event relaxing, exercising, or working through some of the feelings that might get in the way of a good time.

During the visit, avoid those foods, activities, and conversation topics which are certain to upset your moods. If your family insists on bringing up subjects you don't want to discuss, either tell them that issue is off-limits or else move away from the discussion and engage yourself in something more satisfying. If your relatives tease you for doing exercises or avoiding sweet desserts at a get-together, let them tease you, and don't waste your energy trying to convert them to your health habits.

Taking good care of yourself during a family visit could be the difference between another tense encounter and a satisfying connection with your relatives. Failing to do all that is within your power to remain healthy during a family get-together may cause you to feel more sluggish and moody than necessary.

For example, in Julia's daily life she begins each morning with thirty minutes of gentle aerobics and stretching exercises. Otherwise, she knows she won't be at her best the rest of the day. Yet when she visits her in-laws during each holiday season, Julie invariably overeats, forgets to exercise, and then begins to feel vulnerable and testy. She admits, "For years I put the blame on my husband and his parents for not permitting me to exercise and for serving so much heavy food. Yet I know I'm the one who needs to focus on my health during those stressful visits. No one else can do it for me."

This year, Julia made sure she watched what she ate, exercised each day, and took some quiet time for herself during the visit with her husband's family. According to her, the difference was substantial. She recalls, "Taking charge of the situation, at least in terms of remaining healthy, made me feel more like an adult woman and not a cooped-up child this time. They can do what they do and argue with each other all they want, but I still can feel healthy if I make that my priority."

Each of us knows what keeps us healthy and what tends to make us feel tired or oversensitive. During your next visit with your relatives, see how much better you can feel simply by nurturing yourself during the visit. Even if your relatives don't change their behavior at all, you can change the way you enjoy the visit by how well you take care of your health and emotional needs.

4. *You might improve a bad situation if you start noticing what you appreciate about this difficult person rather than only what you detest.* If you and a certain family member are in the habit of noticing only what's wrong about each other and never what's right, is it any wonder you don't get along? To improve the situation, you may need to start remembering this person's good qualities and making sure he or she realizes what's worthy of respect about you, too.

Here's an exercise that has worked successfully for many people, even though most were reluctant to try it at first. It's called "Three Appreciations" and can be used during any phone call or visit in which you and another person have fallen into the habit of criticizing and judging each other.

The instructions are:

—When you notice both of you are giving too much advice and criticism, or when you want to prevent your usual bickering, begin the next conversation with the statement, "How about if we try something different? Let's see if we can say three things we both appreciate about each other. Then let's wait and see if it makes a difference in the way we relate."

—Next, decide who goes first. Then while one person listens without interrupting, the other person describes his or her three appreciations of the listener. No mixed messages are allowed, such as, "I think you're attractive but you've put on some weight lately," or "I like when you do things for others but you've been self-absorbed lately." In this exercise, only unrestricted positive appreciations are permitted. This might be your one opportunity to uncover what you like and respect about this person despite all your differences.

—After one person has given three appreciations, switch and have the other person give her or his positive feelings. Don't rush the exercise. Let both sides have plenty of time and let each listener take in and savor each compliment.

—Finally, notice if the three appreciations change the way you relate to each other. Does it make you both a little less impatient and judgmental with one another? Are you both a little more relaxed after having shared some kind words? Does remembering what you like about this person make it easier to accept the parts you don't like?

For example, when Sally and her stepfather Jonathan did this exercise for the first time, something interesting happened. For years Sally had remained distant and cold with regard to the man her mother married when Sally was nineteen. Even though Sally wanted her mother to be happy, she couldn't bring herself to show Jonathan much warmth.

When Sally began to work through her emotional baggage regarding her stepfather, several insights occurred. First, Sally realized there was still some leftover anger that Sally's mother hadn't done more to save her first marriage to Sally's father. Also, Sally resented the fact that her stepfather had two daughters whom he treated like spoiled princesses. Ever since Jonathan's first wife died, he had put all of his attention on his two "little girls," who still acted like little girls even though they were in their late twenties like Sally.

After she wrote out her resentments in a letter she promised not to send, Sally felt a lot less hostile toward her stepfather. She describes, "I began to feel empathy for Jonathan and my Mom. They both want so badly for us to be one big happy family. I realized how hard it must be for them having lost a partner and still not knowing for sure if their second try is going to succeed."

A week later, Sally called to speak to her mother, but Jonathan answered the phone and told Sally her mother was out with friends. Normally this would have been an awkward moment, with Sally not wanting to be too friendly to Jonathan and he not wanting to seem too nosy by asking her very much about her life.

Yet this time, Sally tried the "Three Appreciations" exercise I had suggested. Telling her stepfather she had something interesting they might enjoy, Sally described the instructions to him and then added, "I think it's about time we started to feel a little less anxious around each other and I've been told this might help. We'll never be quite like father and daughter, but that doesn't mean we can't relax and be ourselves with each other."

Despite some nervousness on both their parts, Sally and Jonathan each listed three appreciations about the other person. Sally talked about Jonathan's creativity and success in his work, his sense of humor, and his understanding patience with her Mom.

Jonathan listed Sally's honesty and courage, her enthusiasm for the arts, and her being a healthy and strong role model for his daughters. By the time Sally and Jonathan finally got off the phone, they had bridged a good part of the distance between them. Instead of remaining cautious rivals, they had begun to develop a mutual respect that would make family get-togethers more relaxed and enjoyable.

No matter how bleak or strained your relationship with a certain family member looks at the present time, you will be surprised at how much unspoken warmth is stored inside you. While you may not get immediate improvements in your relationship, any progress you make in easing your tensions can take a huge load off your shoulders. If you are creative and persistent, eventually you will find a way to feel good about your time with this admittedly challenging person.

Part Three:
Completing a Relationship with Someone
Who Is Unavailable or No Longer Living

In many families, the most difficult challenge is not the everyday conflicts with current relatives but the unfinished business we have with a family member who died or abandoned you a long time ago. How do you work through your unspoken feelings about a parent, child, sibling, or other relative who died too soon? How do you let go of your unresolved conflicts with a close family member who is alive but cannot be reached any longer?

For example, Molly is a forty-year-old woman who hasn't seen her father since she was a small child. While she believes he's still alive, she doesn't know for sure because there has been no word from him for many years. Even though Molly doesn't like to talk about her father and prefers not to think about him, she knows she carries a host of unexpressed feelings of love and hate for this man who was so important in her life. How can she resolve her issues with him if he's not available?

Jack has a different unresolved issue with a family member he can't confront in person. When Jack was growing up, his parents taught him repeatedly that it was his responsibility to take care of his younger brothers and sisters. Even as an adult, Jack felt responsible whenever something bad happened to any of his younger siblings. Recently, when his younger sister became ill and died suddenly, Jack was devastated. He needs to resolve his feelings of guilt and sadness, yet he feels at a loss because he can't communicate with his younger sister any longer. What can he do to work through his loss and get on with his life while still acknowledging the responsibility he feels inside for his younger siblings?

Freda has yet another unresolved relationship with a family member who is no longer living. When Freda was a young child, her mother died and her father relied on his own mother to raise Freda. For years, Freda felt closer to her grandmother than to anyone else in the world. Over the years, Freda moved farther away from her hometown yet still wrote and visited her grandmother often. Although it's been three years since her grandmother died, Freda still hasn't felt resolved about losing this important person. Is there any way she can work through those feelings and finally feel a sense of completion with her grandmother?

THE CHANCE TO BE HEARD

In recent years, I have seen hundreds of women and men work through their unresolved issues with a family member who is unavailable or no longer living by using the following technique. You can try it on your own or with a supportive friend or counselor. Making sure you won't be interrupted for at least a half hour, unplug the phones, and put a "Do Not Disturb" sign on your door. Take a few moments to relax and unwind. Think about the last time you saw or spoke to this person who is no longer around. If possible, have on hand a photograph of him or her that you can look at during this exercise. (Note: This exercise has been used effectively not only for completing a relationship with a family member from the past but also with a spouse, lover, business partner, or friend who is physically, but not emotionally, gone from your life.)

With the photograph of this person in front of you, or with an image of her or him in your mind, take a few moments to get your unexpressed positive and negative feelings out of your system. Either by writing on several sheets of paper or by visualizing yourself talking to this person, imagine that you are able to communicate and be understood as you complete the following:

> Something I never got the chance to thank you for in person . . .
>
> Something I needed from you that you couldn't give me . . .
>
> Something I wish I could have shared with you since the time you left . . .
>
> Something you and I never fully resolved that needs to be cleared up now . . .
>
> Something I always wanted to hear from you which I need to hear right now . . .
>
> Something I want you to know that I've never told you before . . .
>
> Something you have given me that I will always cherish . . .

Quite often we kid ourselves into thinking that just because someone is out of our physical life they have also left our emotional life. In most cases, however, when a close family member or other significant person dies or leaves us, there are many unresolved emotions that can begin to take a toll on our spirit if we don't work them out.

The above exercise is one that I personally have used several times to resolve my strong emotions after losing someone dear to me. It has been most helpful in the gradual process of recovering from the death of my mother when I was fourteen. Since she died when I was so young, I never had the chance to tell her many of the things I needed to tell her. There were many happy and painful experiences I wanted to talk to her about. Despite my love for her, there was also anger I needed to express because she left me when I needed her.

Even though it might seem strange to some people to be talking to a photograph or an imagined memory of a person who is no longer around, this simple technique can release a flood of outdated guilt, sadness, and discomfort from your system. After I did this exercise a few times with my mother in mind, I felt a renewed sense of love for her and acceptance of her death. Instead of being troubled by the loss or resentful at life for being so unfair, I worked through the angry feelings and once again felt energized to carry on. Only after healing my unresolved feelings in this way did I feel less burdened by the tears I shed and more aware of the gifts she gave me.

If you have someone from your past with whom you have never been able to resolve your differences or express your feelings of love and anger, now is a good time to start. There is nothing more cleansing than working through your feelings toward someone whose impact on your life is still being seen. You don't need to carry your conflicts with this person forever. Healing the hurt inside can free you to improve your current family and love relationships.

Renewing Your Sense of Meaning and Purpose

6

> It is not required of you
> to finish the task of repairing the world,
> neither are you to be exempt from it.
> —Traditional Hebrew saying

Several years ago I counseled a woman in her late forties named Roberta, who had three children and a thriving career. A few weeks before I met her, Roberta was told by two physicians that she was suffering from a terminal illness and had only a few months to live. This intelligent and dynamic woman had very little time remaining to solve her unfinished business with her children, her ex-husband, her family, and primarily with herself.

Like many people, Roberta had waited until the very end to start asking the most important questions all of us must address sooner or later—"What meaning does my life have?" "Could I have done more to make my time on Earth count in the long run?" "Has my life enriched the lives of others, especially my loved ones?"

Searching for answers to these and other spiritual questions is no easy task. For many like Roberta, the search is made more difficult because of bad previous experiences—emotional baggage if you will—having to do with religion. In Roberta's case, her discomfort with religion and spirituality stemmed from being raised in a very strict, dogmatic household in which Roberta's curious questions about faith were belittled and certain male authority figures claimed to have all the answers.

Roberta described how, "When I was young, no one encouraged me to look to religion as a source of inner strength or personal growth. In my family and in our community, religion was something people got angry about. There were rules to follow and duties to perform, but they seemed so arbitrary to me. I saw too much fear and hypocrisy attached to religion, so I tried to keep my distance from anyone who reminded me of the zealots I grew up with."

During Roberta's final months, her lifelong alienation from spirituality was hard for her to resolve. Like so many other people, her bad experiences with religion had forced her to suppress a crucial part of herself. Each of us has a rational side, a creative side, an emotional side, and a spiritual side. Yet for many who have had few or no positive experiences with religion and spirituality, their inner search for meaning remains underdeveloped or shut down. Only at the very end of their lives do they seek desperately for a sense of meaning and a reconnection with some source of higher power. Too often that important search begins too late and accomplishes too little.

As Roberta confided shortly before her death, "I now wish I had worked through my antagonism toward religion a long time ago. I think I've always been a deeply spiritual and curious person, but I never let myself take my questions about God or inner purpose too seriously. As a result, I spent a lot of time not knowing what I was living for. I felt disconnected and alone, without the spiritual support I'm still trying to develop."

Missing Out

When you look at your own life, to what extent are you in the same dilemma that Roberta was in? In what ways are you held back from fully exploring your spiritual questions? To what degree are you still missing out because of negative prior experiences with people who told you that unless you believed and practiced *their way,* you had no right to call yourself a spiritual or religious person? To what extent are you still rebelling against the shoulds and oughts of your upbringing?

When people lose touch with their spiritual side, it's usually because they didn't fit in with the strict religious crowd of their early years or they wanted to fit in with the nonreligious secular crowd of their adult life. Regardless of the origins of one's alienation from spirituality, the results are similar. Losing your spiritual focus can create a feeling of emptiness and isolation, especially when times are difficult or you are faced with a personal tragedy. Finding your way in the world without a sense of meaning and purpose is like hiking in the woods with no map, compass, or sense of direction—you never know if you're making good choices or if you're lost with no grasp of the larger picture.

For years, men and women turned away from spirituality and put their faith in science and technology. Yet once again, intelligent people are realizing that science has its limits. Even today, there are many things that can't be explained by reason or science and still require a sense of faith or belief. In addition, the uncontrolled worship of science has led to the possibility of nuclear destruction, the dangers of genetic engineering, a greatly dehumanized workplace, and the continued poisoning of our air, water, and environment because of the long-held belief that science is "Making Life Better Through Chemistry."

In today's high-pressure world, many people are returning to more basic questions, those usually associated with religion and spirituality—"Are love and family more important than the constant pursuit of success?" "Aren't there better ways to feed the hungry and find shelter for the homeless?" "Isn't there something more I could be doing with my life to make an impact on the things I feel are wrong?"

It's easy to fall into a routine that causes you to miss out on the spiritual element of life. When that happens, everything looks like a struggle and your life seems to be an endless treadmill with no hope for relief. Living without a sense of direction or purpose often means striving for results that feel empty or worthless once you have them.

On the other hand, when you renew your awareness of the spiritual dimension in life, you begin to notice things you had forgotten were right in front of you. For example, your children look different when you think of them as part of a miraculous chain of creation and not just an expensive extension of your ego. Quite often, your capacity to love and share your compassion with others increases in direct proportion to your sense of meaning and purpose. Your sense of fulfillment also is enhanced by knowing the path you are on. When your eyes are open to the spiritual element, the beauty of nature and the stunning sight of a golden sunset make you stop and realize you are part of something larger than your daily crises.

The Psychological Importance of the Spiritual Quest

At this point, you might be asking why a book on psychology and emotional baggage is devoting a chapter to the subject of religion and spiritual renewal. Certainly, there are easier subjects to talk about, ones that might bring up less controversy. Religion is a topic about which most people disagree vehemently, and about which many people become self-righteous and intolerant.

So I need to ask you at this point to be patient and open-minded. The next several pages will explore why spirituality plays such an important role in our lives and why so many people get turned off or turned away from exploring their own spiritual paths. I have seen repeatedly that a search for meaning and purpose is one of the most important fresh starts a person can make. Yet too often the emotional baggage we carry based on previous disappointments and disagreements with religion holds us back.

Most people don't realize that the word *psychology* comes from the root words *psyche* and *logos,* which mean "the study of the soul" or "the science of the spirit." Too often psychology has been so concerned with proving itself as a science that it lost sight of its crucial role—to address the spiritual and soulful concerns of people, to explain what supports the human spirit and what detracts from it.

When I was an undergraduate at Kenyon College in Ohio, I was amazed at how sterile and scientific many of my psychology courses were. Rats, pigeons, statistics, and standardized tests—not exactly an exploration of the human spirit.

Then I was fortunate to find a teacher who asked me to read one of the lesser known psychotherapists, a Holocaust survivor named Viktor Frankl, who wrote several important works, including *Man's Search for Meaning*.

Briefly stated, Frankl's work with people both in the concentration camps and afterward led him to the conclusion that when we lose our sense of meaning and purpose in life, psychological and physical ailments are more likely to occur. At the same time, when you or I renew our sense of moving on a spiritual path or having a deeper purpose in life, even the worst tragedies and most difficult challenges can be faced with a sense of dignity, hope, and inner strength.

I was moved by Frankl's story of how he survived several near-death experiences in the concentration camps and how he retained his sense of meaning and purpose despite losing his father, mother, brother, and wife to the Nazis. These stories of compassion and inner strength were especially significant to me since my own family lost many members in the camps and the gas chambers.

Part of my becoming a psychologist was to understand not only what makes human beings mistreat each other but to find out how we can restore the sacredness of life even after suffering painful losses. As I see it, the job of a psychologist—one who studies the human spirit—is to help individuals find and express their unique purpose in life. When someone comes to a psychologist after suffering a painful setback or experiencing a loss of hope, it is the psychologist's responsibility to work with that person in finding his or her unique strengths and reasons for living.

When I talk of "renewal" in this chapter, I'm not referring to the "give me your money and you'll be saved" types of blind faith you sometimes see on television. The renewal that many thoughtful people search for these days is more subtle and occurs on a deeper level. It is the fresh start that happens when a person rediscovers the important purpose why he or she is here. It is the realization of what brings you true satisfaction—when you look at your loved ones, your work, your commitments and your deepest beliefs with a renewed sense of, "Yes, this is why I get up in the morning."

For many people, that essential renewal can't take place until they first work through their bad experiences with religion. They won't regain a clear sense of spiritual purpose as long as they are carrying unresolved baggage about previous disappointments or tragedies that turned them away from believing in anything beside themselves. To resume a spiritual quest you first have to resolve what previously disrupted your journey.

Sorting Out Your Positive and Negative Experiences

When you look back to your childhood and your early adult years, what were your most memorable experiences with religion and spirituality? What enjoyable or dreadful moments can you recall about religious services, holiday get-togethers, and rites of passage such as births, deaths, baptisms, bar mitzvahs, and weddings? What good and bad conversations did you share with grandparents, parents, clergy, teachers, roommates, and others who made you more interested or less interested in religion?

It also helps in rediscovering your spirituality to look at the twists and turns your journey has taken in the past. When did you feel close to God or a higher source of power? When did you experience a sense of alienation or resentment toward your faith or your earlier ideas about religion? When did you feel like an insider at your church, synagogue, or religious group? When did you feel like an outsider?

For the past seven years I've discussed questions like these with hundreds of women and men from all walks of life and religious backgrounds who volunteered to talk about their spiritual needs as part of a program sponsored by the National Conference of Christians and Jews. Despite all our differences, I've found that many of us share certain similar experiences. For example, see how many of the following ring true for you.

When exploring the twists and turns of their spiritual lives:

Most people can recall at least one beloved relative (often a grandparent or immigrant relative) who seemed to have a heartfelt connection to his or her religious tradition. Some individuals felt a sense of envy for those whose strong spiritual center guided and supported them during the struggles of their lives.

In your own family or background, who are the people you've met that seemed to have a warm, heartfelt, and positive sense of their religious or spiritual traditions?

What was it about the way they acted (their conversations, their rituals, the foods they made, or the feelings they passed along) that gave you a sense of their spirituality?

On the other hand, most people also remember feeling resentful that they were forced to perform certain rituals that they opposed or didn't understand. Many felt belittled or ostracized by religious zealots in their families or neighborhoods who said, in essence, "I won't respect you as a person unless you believe and practice the same way I believe and practice."

In your own life, who have been the people who tried to impose their religious beliefs and practices on you? What were the incidents that made you resent or want to pull away from religion?

Many people have admired certain highly religious

women and men (either public figures like Martin Luther King, Jr., Dorothy Day, and Mahatma Gandhi, or less well-known people in one's own community) whose passion and service to others came from a strong sense of spiritual purpose.

In your own background, who are the religious and ethical role models you've wanted to emulate or follow?

When have you been inspired by someone's act of courage or compassion for others?

Many felt strongly that religious study would be important to help their children's moral development, yet they resisted too much spiritual exploration in their own lives. Some felt embarrassed at times about admitting their beliefs or sense of purpose to others, as though being cynical and skeptical was "sophisticated" while feeling a strong connection to a higher source was "unsophisticated."

In what ways have you felt uncomfortable admitting your spiritual questions or religious beliefs to others?

In what ways have you pretended to be "too sophisticated" to have concerns about meaning, purpose, and the nature of things? Why do you think you've felt that way?

In many cases a person resumed a spiritual path after encountering a difficult time, such as a divorce, a career setback, the death of a loved one, or a serious illness.

At what times in your life did you begin thinking more seriously about spiritual and religious questions? What are some of the unresolved issues you still have concerns about?

Quite often a person stopped exploring his or her spirituality during times of stability, when day-to-day concerns dominated that person's life, or when a spouse or lover disapproved of religious topics. In many cases, people who outwardly seemed oblivious to spiritual concerns inwardly carried a host of unspoken questions and curiosities.

What might be your next step for exploring your spirituality?

What do you need to resolve about the religious experiences (or lack of religious experiences) in your upbringing?

What do you miss or wish you could add to your spiritual life?

Taking the Next Step

From talking with so many people about their religious backgrounds, I began to realize each of us has our own unique struggle to work through the bad experiences that turn us away from our spirituality. Each of us has to search deeply for a sense of purpose that we can take into our most significant relationships, work situations, life crises, and personal challenges. Even if your background consisted of little or no healthy examples of spiritual search and inner strength, it's not too early or too late for you to begin developing your own sense of renewal.

For some people, returning to an awareness of the spiritual element in life means going back to a religion she or he left a long time ago. Quite often people who turned away from the faith and practice of their families find that, as adults, they can sort out what they like from what they don't like about the religion. Instead of continuing their rebellion and running away from the religion they grew up with, they go back to the same group or denomination and help to institute changes that make the church or synagogue more responsive to their needs.

In other cases, people who rediscover their spirituality look beyond organized religion to other groups that offer different ways of contacting a higher source. Still others find their spiritual connection in nature, by writing in a journal, by meditating alone or in a community, or by discovering meaningful answers in books, talks, and rituals that come from a variety of spiritual or metaphysical backgrounds.

Regardless of where you look for partners and supporters in your spiritual quest, make sure you avoid the same mistakes you made before and that you watch out for the false promises and dishonest practices that are so rampant in today's world. I remember when I first moved from the East Coast to California, I received a long-distance phone call from an old friend who said, "You must be bored out there. It's so laid back and relaxed compared to the northeast."

Based on my first few weeks in California, I had to disagree and explain, "It's not laid back at all. On every corner, at every party, and in every newspaper and magazine there are countless numbers of gurus, groups, fakers, and followers, each telling you that they alone can change your life instantly and forever. With everyone so busy trying to change, I haven't met anyone who has time to relax."

The Elements of a Renewed Spirituality

If you want to move forward in your spiritual search without getting swept away by the demands of true-believers and arm-twisters, there are several things to keep in mind. On the following pages you will find some basic guidelines for exploring your spiritual side in a psychologically healthy manner.

I have given these elements as guidelines to people from very different religions, yet I have been told they work just as well whether your background and beliefs are Catholic, Protestant, Jewish, Buddhist, Muslim, Hindu, or "none of the above." Primarily I offer them to you as food for thought. If at any time you feel lost or stuck in a rut on your spiritual path, look to these elements as suggestions of the next step forward you might take in your spiritual growth.

A Sense of Sacred Space

You and I both know that if there is a higher power, He or She exists everywhere and you don't have to go to a certain special place to find that spiritual connection. Yet we human beings are funny. We forget to notice the sacredness of life until we are reminded of it by certain sights and places that shake us back to our senses.

What are those places in your own life that make you step out of the mundane world and remember the larger picture? For some people, a sense of the holy comes from a trip to India, Israel, Italy, or some other location where the spiritual energy is vivid and powerful. Many others find a sense of the infinite when they walk in nature or see a breathtaking site such as a mountaintop view, a rushing river, a bucolic meadow, or the vastness of the ocean.

What many people fail to realize is that sacred spaces may be closer to your everyday world than you might imagine. For example, here are two illustrations to give you some ideas of how to find a sense of sacredness close to where you live or work:

> John is a corporate executive in Manhattan who used to keep his business life and his spiritual life completely separate. Recently, he was offered a new position for

more money, but the job also entailed spending more time away from his family.

The day before he was supposed to make up his mind and respond to the offer, John was returning from lunch when he got caught in a sudden rainstorm. He describes what happened, "I was walking back from a lunch meeting along Fifth Avenue when it began to come down in buckets. Trying not to get soaked, I stopped into St. Patrick's Cathedral and watched the sheets of rain pouring down. As the storm continued, I sat down in one of the pews and began listening to my thoughts. I'd never before taken time out of my busy day to meditate or seek spiritual guidance, but that day I weighed my job offer slowly and with a seriousness I rarely brought to business decisions. By the time I left the Cathedral, I knew what I had to do. Since that afternoon, I've taken many opportunities to stop by the Cathedral and listen to my thoughts. It's one of the few places in midtown where a person can get a fresh perspective on something that's on your mind."

Tracy is a mother of two and a home-based business-woman. Like many who work at home, she finds herself constantly being interrupted by phone calls, the pressures of raising and carpooling her children, and the struggles of a business. According to Tracy, "After a while it got so hectic I started resenting my kids for distracting me from my work and resenting the business for taking me away from my kids."

Then Tracy decided to try something different. She redecorated a small storage room in her home and turned it into a quiet place for relaxation and daily centering. She describes how, "At first it seemed like a good idea, but then my doubts sprung up. Was I becoming too self-indulgent by wanting a 'room of one's own'? Were the kids going to respect my need for a quiet space? Was my husband going to laugh at me or call me a holy roller?

"Then when the room was redecorated and I explained the ground rules to everyone that this was a special place for quiet thinking, I was surprised by how little resistance I got. Sure, the kids tested me a few times and my husband made a few remarks, but eventually that small room became a place for tuning out the noise and listening to the feelings inside."

Other examples of sacred spaces used by people to regain their spiritual sense in the middle of difficult times include the following: sitting under a tree in a city park; taking a walk through a rural area or along a waterfront; writing in your journal in a coffee shop or restaurant that doesn't rush its customers; visiting an art museum; reading in a public library; going to a nearby spiritual retreat center, convent, religious camp, or meditation center; resting in a rooftop garden; closing the door to your office or study; or joining a study group or course on spirituality.

In many cases, people think that sacred spaces and a reconnection with one's spirituality are far away or hard to find. It reminds me of a story told by Elie Wiesel in his book *Souls on Fire*. According to the tale, there was once a man named Eizik who was having trouble paying his bills, keeping up his responsibilities as a father, and finding his direction in life. Then one night he had a strange dream that a huge treasure waited for him in a far-off city he had never visited.

While Eizik tried to ignore the dream, it kept coming back to him night after night. Finally, he decided to journey on foot to the faraway city and look for his treasure. When he at last reached the spot that looked like the place in his dream, he found it was guarded by soldiers. Eizik was afraid his search had been a mistake.

The captain of the soldiers suspected Eizik was a spy and demanded to know what he was looking for. Eizik told him the truth—about the dream, the journey, and the treasure. The captain burst out laughing and advised Eizik not to believe in dreams. To prove his point, the captain told Eizik about one of his own dreams that he, too, had a treasure waiting for him far away under a stove in a house owned by some man named Eizik whom the guard said he had never met. The captain knew the dream was absurd so he ignored it.

Eizik returned to his home and, needless to say, discovered a treasure under the stove in his own home. That's the discovery many spiritual people take a long time to find—the awareness that searching wide and far for answers can often lead you astray when, in fact, the treasures you seek might be in your own home, your own religious tradition, your own inner wisdom.

A Sense of Sacred Time

A second important element in many spiritual traditions and paths is the search for a release from the constraints of time. For most people, time feels like an enemy. Rushing to an appointment, time seems to be moving too quickly. Looking in the mirror at lines and wrinkles, you worry that time is creeping up on you. There never seems to be enough hours in the day. Or you've got too much time on your hands and you don't know how to make it worthwhile.

To break out of this rut of feeling oppressed by time, most spiritual traditions contain several ways to step out of time, to transcend the present moment and go beyond the limitations of seconds, hours, and years to something more sacred. By sacred time, I am referring to those moments when you essentially let go of your anxious thoughts and move to a deeper level of awareness. This deeper level might give you a sense of inner strength and continuity that your daily life has lost. It might provide you with a feeling of renewal and purpose that you can bring to your life's challenges. Stepping out of time allows you to rediscover what really matters and what your inner voice might be trying to tell you.

Here are some examples of how religions achieve this sense of sacred time:

—In Native American prayer rituals, the sense of connection with nature, with higher spirits, and with ancestors provides a direct link between the present moment and the invisible but still viable past.

—In the Hindu and Buddhist traditions, the present moment is often viewed as a deceptive illusion while the energies of past, present, and future are seen as acting together in an endless chain of events.

—In Christianity, when a believer thinks deeply about the birth, death, or life of Jesus, he or she is stepping out of time and experiencing Christ's love and guidance in the present moment. Even though Jesus spent only thirty-three years on Earth, to a believing Christian the presence of Christ transcends time and provides inner strength and an ethical role model on a daily basis.

—In the Islamic Sufi tradition, dance and music are important vehicles for breaking free of the present moment and envisioning a sacred time of universal peace. Music, dance, and art are used in many traditions as a similar vehicle.

—In Judaism, the Sabbath is one example of how Jews attempt to step out of time and reexperience the sacredness of life. By lighting candles, blessing wine and bread, sharing songs and dancing with family and friends, the Sabbath celebrates the divine presence that exists beyond time.

—In most religions, there are historic events and sacred days that ask believers to step out of time and renew their sense of meaning and purpose. On these holidays, men and women stop their daily habits and participate instead in rituals that reconnect them with their traditions and their search for meaning. If you look hard enough, you will find that behind nearly every religious ritual is an attempt to transcend the meaninglessness of modern life and restore a sense of purpose and direction.

In your own life, what are some of the ways you have developed to step out of time and reconnect with the spiritual element? Here are some examples to give you possible ideas:

—Many experience a sense of "timelessness" when they are in love or share a heartfelt activity with another person. If you have ever looked into someone's eyes and felt a tremendous wave of appreciation and at-one-ness with that person, you know the feeling of stepping out of time.

—Others experience a sense of transcendence when they let themselves settle into the rhythms and beauty of nature. After several days on a river, in the wilderness, or by the ocean, you may have a sense of being at one with nature. During those moments you lose your sense of separateness and experience what Thoreau had in mind when he said, "My purpose in going to Walden Pond was not to live cheaply, but to transact some private business . . . to step to the beat of a different drummer . . . with the fewest obstacles."

—Still others break free of the stresses of time by stopping and listening to their inner voice at several intervals during the day. For example, if you take time out before each meal to be still for a moment or say a silent prayer, it changes the way you eat. Otherwise, when you gobble down healthy or low-calorie food in a hurry it's not healthy. You can improve your chances of becoming fit by relaxing first and reconnecting with a sense of inner peace.

—Another opportunity to step out of time and change your sense of hurriedness into a relaxed gratitude is by praying or meditating during spontaneous moments during the day. When you notice something positive or beautiful, acknowledge it with a silent prayer of thanks. When you have a few moments to spare, meditate instead of worrying or planning. When you notice your mind is racing, take ten or twenty minutes to relax, unwind, and reconnect with a sense of the infinite.

—Finally, there are many people who step out of time when they are fully experiencing the present moment. Whether you are playing with your child, riding a bicycle, writing in your journal, jogging, dancing, doing yoga or aikido, working at your craft, making love, or sitting in a chair, use each opportunity you have to be fully in the here-and-now. Once again, you may find you don't have to travel too far outside your own environment in order to experience a sense of transcendence. The divine presence is not something you go searching for, but which you find within.

A Sense of Purpose

A third critical element of spirituality that we each need is a sense of meaning and purpose. Too often, however, other people try to impose on you what they think your sense of purpose should be. From the time you are born, people are forever trying to distract you from your inner purpose and assign you what their values are. Unfortunately, many individuals use up so much energy rebelling against or being sidetracked by the expectations of others that you don't follow through on your own heartfelt sense of purpose and direction.

Now is a good time to take a fresh look at what your inner sense of purpose and meaning might be. The more you understand about your special gifts and unique opportunities to live a life of meaning, the more likely you are to feel a sense of being on the right path. Here are some techniques to consider:

1. There are many creative ways to uncover a stronger sense of meaning and direction for your own life. One way, suggested by Viktor Frankl, is simply to ask yourself, "Why haven't I committed suicide?" Even if the question sounds morbid or absurd, when you think about it seriously you will discover there are specific reasons your being here is important and worthwhile.

Maybe the reason you don't end it all is because of your love for your children, your work, your creativity, your sense of discovery, or your commitment to a cause or a volunteer activity. Maybe you just have a sense of wanting to follow through on the hard work you've done to become a person capable of love and sharing your special gifts of insight and compassion. Possibly you are waiting to be used for a higher purpose and your moment hasn't arrived yet. Probably you know there are ways you contribute to specific individuals, even if those efforts are not often acknowledged or appreciated.

2. Another creative method of recognizing your deeper purpose is to write your own obituary, looking back from a point in the distant future. What will be the important elements of your life that in hindsight will allow you or others to say, "That was a worthwhile person. This person had something to share and will be missed." Quite often when you do this exercise, it stimulates ideas of how to make your life more purposeful while there's still plenty of time left. If you're not satisfied with the contribution you've made thus far, you still have a chance to build a life that makes a loving impact on your corner of the world.

3. Yet another way to explore your meaning in life is to take note of the different ways you have been called to be of service to others. Here are some questions that can help you refocus on your sense of purpose.

—What are the moments in your life when someone has come to you for help and you were able to give something valuable? What recent opportunities have presented themselves for you to get involved?

—What are the strengths, lessons, and experiences you've acquired over a lifetime that might be useful to others if you found a way to share your insights with them? What are the special gifts and talents you've developed that you can now offer to help others?

—What are the injustices and serious problems you've encountered that need your ideas and your energy? What situations could you help improve so that others won't be forced to suffer in ways you or your ancestors were forced to suffer?

This technique of constantly asking yourself, "How can I be of service?," could be the source of many rewarding ideas and meaningful projects. Clearly you will need to make sure you don't overcommit yourself or become burned out. Yet you will never be lacking for meaning and purpose if you remember to face each difficult time in your life with the attitude, "How can I turn this into something that will be of service to others?"

For example, Arthur's story illustrates the importance of stepping back from a personal crisis and asking yourself, "How can I turn this experience into something that will help others and get myself back on track?"

A sensitive and intelligent man in his late thirties who has worked in a number of fields, Arthur recently thought he had finally found his career direction. Working as a creative consultant to a computer software company, Arthur felt he at last had a job with a future and some security.

Then an industry-wide slump in the computer software business put the firm Arthur worked for into bankruptcy. Arthur was devastated. For several weeks, he berated himself that this once again proved he was irresponsible, a flake, someone who would never find a worthwhile direction.

However, when Arthur turned his setback into a question—How can I use this experience to be of service? —several constructive ideas came to mind. He thought about forming a consulting business to help retrain people who had lost their jobs. He considered writing a book about how to take care of your doubts and critical voices when you're out of work. He also looked into volunteer activities that could give him a sense of purpose and satisfaction while he was looking for another job. Choosing carefully from several volunteer opportunities, Arthur decided to work for free while he sent out resumes and waited to hear from prospective employers.

Working four afternoons a week at a local hospital as a volunteer, Arthur rediscovered a sense of self-worth that had been taken from him when he'd lost his job. He describes, "Even though it was frustrating applying to computer software firms and getting rejected, when I'd go to my volunteer job each afternoon I felt like a human being again. Working with people who care about what they're doing and helping people who really appreciate a responsive person can make all the difference. I stopped second-guessing myself and started feeling once again I was here for a purpose."

After six months as a volunteer, Arthur was asked to take on a new position as the coordinator of volunteer services. Even though he had thought his future was in the computer software field, he discovered his satisfaction came from working with people. What began as a career setback had turned into a rewarding opportunity. Arthur admits, "I don't know if this is a forever position, but I do know that I've learned a lot about myself and what I'm capable of accomplishing if I trust my instincts and keep focusing on things that feel worthwhile."

Another example of how being of service to others can turn a setback into an opportunity is illustrated by Marjorie's case. A fifty-six-year-old woman with four grown children, Marjorie had considered going back to work or doing something useful after her youngest child graduated from college and got married. But like many people who have been out of the work world for a long time, Marjorie felt unsure of her skills and hesitant to rush into something that might turn out badly.

Then a personal tragedy shook her life up even more. Marjorie's husband died suddenly of a heart attack, leaving Marjorie alone and seriously depressed. Even after two years as a widow, Marjorie wasn't sure how she was going to regain her sense of purpose and direction. She admitted, "I've always been a relatively productive and happy person. But these days nothing feels comfortable or right to get involved with. My friends keep suggesting I join a counseling group. My kids keep giving me leads for jobs they hear about. I feel guilty for staying home, but there's a part of me that just doesn't have the confidence to take on a new challenge right now."

When Marjorie talked to me about her problem, I asked her to think about what other passions she'd had in her lifetime besides her husband and her family. At first nothing came to mind for her. Then I asked her the same question in a different way—What things had Marjorie witnessed in her life that upset her or made her wish there were a better way?

Something about that question made her perk up and seem more animated. With conviction in her voice, Marjorie told me how upset she'd been for a long time about latchkey children in her neighborhood, young boys and girls who came home each night from school to an empty house because both parents worked or they lived with only one parent, who worked. Marjorie explained, "I've always supported the idea of women working and I realize that in many families both partners need to have jobs to make ends meet. But it's always upset me to see kids all alone with no supervision, no one to help them with homework, no one to suggest activities other than drinking, smoking cigarettes, taking drugs, or sitting in front of the television set like a zombie."

Gradually over a period of months, Marjorie expanded on her feelings about latchkey children. Not only did she have strong feelings about the problem, but she also began to have enthusiasm and good ideas about solutions that could be enacted in her own neighborhood. After thinking through her ideas carefully and analyzing various options, Marjorie decided to coordinate and help run a neighborhood drop-in center for school-age children. With the help of a local social service organization and several volunteers from a nearby college, Marjorie established what has become an outstanding after-school facility for neighborhood youths. As a result, she's gradually regained a sense of purpose and satisfaction. After years of having her life on hold, she feels productive and alive again.

In your own life, what are some of the untapped passions and unexpressed gifts you might want to begin thinking about? Even if it doesn't turn into an immediate project, there's no harm in brainstorming with a friend, relative, or counselor about various options you have that would give your life more meaning and fulfillment. Sometimes it means responding to an immediate situation that needs your help. Other times it means recalling a heartfelt interest that you had to postpone or ignore long ago but now could renew successfully. There is no greater satisfaction than to be used for a higher purpose. There is no richer way to live than to know you are being of service to others. We all know the world needs repair; whatever you can do in your own corner of the world is important and worthwhile.

"Activities from the Heart"

Quite often you and I may think about getting involved in something meaningful, yet the time pressures of our work, family responsibilities, and personal life make those involvements unlikely. We wind up saying things like, "I'd get involved if I only had the time," or "I can't take on anymore volunteer activities until I resolve the other priorities in my life."

There's a simpler way to deal with this complex issue. Instead of waiting for the "perfect" moment to do something that helps others and thus boosts your own sense of vitality, begin to look at good deeds as an integral part of your daily life. Each day you can set aside a half hour to follow through on the good ideas you've had about things that matter to you and those you care about. Use that half hour to call, write, or do something for someone who would love to hear from you. During that daily half hour of "Activities from the Heart," write a letter to the editor about an issue you think your local newspaper is failing to cover or is reporting in an insensitive manner. Write a letter to your congressperson or senator about issues that he or she needs to be more involved with. Or simply use that daily half hour to catch up on the reading or preparation work that will allow you to do a better job in your volunteer activities. Rather than viewing your good deeds as a duty or a burden, begin to enjoy them as some of the most worthwhile and enriching parts of your life.

If you set aside at least one half hour a day to do things that are of service to the people and causes you care about, you will be amazed at how much you can accomplish. If you set aside one weekend a month to participate in a volunteer activity that makes someone else's life better and thus adds to your own sense of purpose, you will be rewarded on an emotional level far in excess of the dollar value of your time.

Every year when I look back at what the peak moments of that year were for me, I usually get the most satisfaction and sense of meaning not out of the things I got paid for, but from the special moments that happened simply because I put myself in a situation to be of service to others. Quite often it is a volunteer activity that I wasn't sure I had the time to do, but while doing it something wonderful occurred. Repeatedly I've found that in the process of helping someone else, you discover a part of yourself that you've never fully appreciated before. In many instances, the person you are attempting to help is actually helping and teaching you. You may be giving someone your time, but this person is giving you his or her courage, honesty and hard-earned wisdom.

If you have said or thought recently that you wish you had a stronger sense of meaning and purpose in your life, now is the time to take that first step and get involved in something that stretches the narrow boundaries you've been living within. Some individual or organization needs what you have to offer—in return, you will gain the satisfaction of knowing you have made the world a slightly better place to live.

7

Fencesitters Anonymous

> I won't think of it now ...
> I'll think of it tomorrow.
> —Scarlett O'Hara

First, there was Alcoholics Anonymous. Later, there was Overeaters Anonymous. Now it's time for a new type of support technique for a habit that holds so many of us back—Fencesitters Anonymous.

Even the most decisive men and women have certain areas of their life in which they are sitting on the fence, unable to make a decision or follow through with a commitment. Here are some of the most common examples that might describe you or someone you know:

"I can't decide . . .
  whether to make a long-term commitment."
  whether to end the relationship."
  if I'm ready to have children."
  what do to now that the children are grown."
  whether to look for a new job."
  if I should start my own business."
  whether to look for a new place to live."
  how to fix up where I've been living."
  whether to tell a certain person exactly how I feel."
  how to respond now that this person has told me his or her feelings."
  whether to ask for help and support."
  whether to go it alone."

154

if I should follow through on my good ideas."
if I should wait until I feel more certain."

Most people have good intentions to take the next step forward in an area of their life that has been stuck. But good intentions aren't enough. Just when you need to make a firm commitment and finally get on with it, something happens that causes you to stall or stop.

Why do so many of us procrastinate and stop short of goals we know we want? Why do otherwise productive women and men remain caught on the fence with certain decisions that need to be made? Why do we start out with so much enthusiasm to finish something and then get distracted so easily?

Welcome to Fencesitters Anonymous. This support technique does not require dues, membership forms, or attendance at regular meetings. In fact, if it did, could you imagine how hard it would be for a group of fencesitters and procrastinators to show up each week? The fencesitters would be trying to decide whether or not to attend the meeting. The procrastinators would be finding distractions and reasons to put off going. On some nights, the room would be empty, with everyone finding brilliant excuses not to attend.

Rather than a public gathering, the Fencesitters Anonymous technique I am about to describe can be done in private. In the next several pages, you will discover you are not the only one who stops short of your goals or who puts off making important commitments and decisions. Many intelligent and well-intentioned people suffer from the frustrating habit of stalling and stopping in the middle of an important challenge. Yet through understanding the pattern and working through the habit, there is hope. Even the most chronic fencesitters can get on with their lives if they follow certain techniques that have proven successful for many other individuals.

The Discomforts of Sitting on the Fence Too Long

While you can expect moments of indecision or hesitation whenever you attempt to move forward in your life, for many people the reluctance to get on with things is chronic and debilitating. Here are some actual comments from men and women who were willing to look at the hidden costs of their indecisiveness and procrastination. See how many of these sound familiar about yourself or someone whose fencesitting is affecting your life:

> I keep fluctuating between wanting to change jobs and then not wanting to go through the hassle of changing jobs. It's hard getting rejected when I go for interviews and sometimes finding the new job isn't so much better than the old one.

> I'm stuck on the fence about my primary relationship. One day we're getting along great and I tell myself, "Maybe I should stay," but then we start to get on each other's nerves and I wonder, "Maybe I should go."

> I have good ideas for creative projects but then I get distracted and I never seem to complete them. The worst part is when I see other people finishing projects and developing ideas I had a while back but didn't carry through. I tell myself, "Next time you are going to block out all distractions and get the job done." But next time comes and I get sidetracked again.

> My procrastination problem is that I hold back saying what I'm feeling when it's the right moment. Then by the time I open my mouth, it's too late. I wind up arguing in my head at night with people who are probably enjoying a good night's sleep. If only I could speak my mind right when the conflict is happening instead of taking so much home with me every night.

I'm starting to notice that people I care about are impatient with my habit of saying I'll do something and I don't follow through. When I talk about my plans and good ideas, I can feel their skepticism. I imagine they're thinking, "Here it goes again . . . lots of talk but no action." I don't want to be seen as a flake, but so many times I've stopped short of finishing things that I'm afraid no one is going to believe my word any longer.

When you allow your habit of stalling and stopping to run your life, it not only deprives you of important goals but also diminishes your self-respect. Most procrastinators feel bad about themselves because of their long list of promises not kept.

Sitting on the fence too long can be costly. Quite often you lose the very thing you are trying to keep but can't make up your mind about. For instance, consider the following:

Henry was in love with someone but couldn't make up his mind about living together. The longer Henry remained undecided, the more tension and disagreements entered their relationship. Eventually this person chose to break up with Henry rather than wait forever for him to make up his mind. Like many who lost a relationship because of his or her own hesitation and indecision, Henry was filled with regrets. He wondered often what might have happened if he'd found a way to work through the emotional issues that made him unable to commit.

Deniece spent several months not talking to one of her closest friends because of a heated argument they had after Deniece tried to give her friend unsolicited advice about a relationship. Throughout those months, Deniece kept fluctuating between wanting to reconnect with her friend and wanting to remain angry and defiant. Then Deniece received a piece of shocking news—her friend had been critically injured in a car accident. By the time Deniece reached the hospital in order to patch things up with her friend, it was too late. Deniece was left not only grieving the death of a close friend but regretting how long she'd waited to reestablish communication after an unfortunate argument.

Theresa had been meaning to finish her education and improve her income level for several years, but she kept putting it off. First, it was because of a relationship that required a lot of time and energy. Then it was because Theresa had two small children to raise on her own. Finally, Theresa put off finishing her education because her employer was overcommitted to customers and needed her to work overtime. The longer Theresa put off this goal, which meant a lot to her, the worse she felt about herself and her current situation as a single parent working in a job where she was insufficiently acknowledged. Then one of Theresa's children got sick and required a lot of attention and expensive medical treatments. Theresa no longer had the time or the money to finish her education. What had once been a dream now felt like an impossibility.

The Art of Stalling

If sitting on the fence is so costly, why then do we do it so automatically? Why is it so hard for us to make decisions and take on the challenges in front of us?

I've noticed for a long time that some of the biggest procrastinators and fencesitters are also the most intelligent and creative people. Rather than sticking to one goal, one path to the goal, and no diversions, these talented individuals do an incredible job of creating distractions, detours, and delays that keep them from finishing what they've begun.

In most cases, these distractions and delays are not intentional but come from deep-seated patterns from long ago. Only by understanding the subtle reasons why you have a habit of sitting on the fence can you successfully break the pattern and get on with your life.

There are three overall reasons why people become indecisive and shut down just at the point when they desire to move forward toward a worthwhile goal. You may want to think carefully about your own hesitations in an important area of your life. How similar are your fencesitting patterns to those listed below?

"It Worked Then, Why Isn't It Working Now?"

The first reason why many people procrastinate is because they learned a long time ago that it was safer to stall than to risk the criticism, rejection or disappointment they received from finishing things. For example, have you ever . . .

. . . gotten a lot of support and assistance when you were running way behind schedule, whereas if you had been on time no one would have offered to help?

. . . gotten a lot of attention for not making a decision, not making a commitment, or saving your opinion until the very end? The more someone begged you to "Please make up your mind already," the more powerful and in control you felt.

. . . avoided someone's criticism or disapproval by not completing what he or she might then criticize? The longer you told this person, "I'm not done yet," the longer you put off the inevitable moment when they might tell you it's not good enough.

. . . avoided having to leave a bad but familiar situation that you might not have liked but you weren't sure you could replace with something better? The longer you procrastinated, the more you could blame your dissatisfactions on the old situation rather than on your failure to make something new come to fruition.

From past experiences like these, many of us have learned that stalling and stopping can, at times, save you from getting criticized for finishing something you aren't sure you can do well. Rather than being encouraged to do your best, you may have been belittled or made to believe in your household chores, work assignments, love life, or family relationships that "nothing you do is good enough." Is it any wonder you have learned to avoid making decisions or finishing things when you knew certain people would invariably find fault with whatever decision or completed results you presented to them?

For example, Pamela is an extremely intelligent and warm person who unfortunately grew up with two overly critical parents. In addition, Pamela went to a very strict school where her teachers thought the best way to motivate students was to intimidate, belittle, and criticize everything the students did.

As a survival mechanism with her critical parents and teachers, Pamela learned to be indecisive and procrastinating. The longer she put off making up her mind about something, the longer she could avoid being criticized for her decisions. For example, the longer Pamela stalled in making up her mind about what to wear to school, the more her mother helped out and gave her the attention Pamela rarely got as one of six children. If Pamela picked out her own outfit, her mother would ignore her or criticize her choice. Yet if Pamela appeared to be unable to make a decision or be on time for school, her mother would feel needed and get involved in Pamela's problems.

On a subconscious level, Pamela learned as a young woman that the more helpless and indecisive she acted, the more attention, assistance, and support she got from certain important people. On the other hand, if she acted decisive and competent, she might get ignored, criticized, or told "whatever you do isn't up to standard."

As an adult, however, Pamela discovered that her

learned habit of indecisiveness and procrastination was costing her more than she liked. Several times her pattern of acting helpless, taking far too long to make a not-so-difficult decision, and not completing things got her in hot water with impatient bosses and business partners. She also discovered that when she acted helpless or failed to be decisive around her husband, he would take advantage of her procrastination and make most of their decisions by himself.

Like many fencesitters who learned to be indecisive and procrastinating in order to survive in their critical families, Pamela found that these long-term habits were difficult to change. Even though as an adult she needed to be more decisive and efficient, Pamela had become so accustomed to stalling and stopping that she didn't have the skills or habits to do otherwise. Not until she gradually worked through the emotional reasons why she had learned to become a fencesitter was she ready to start becoming more in charge of her life. Only when she began to notice how much her indecisiveness was costing her did she begin developing new skills for being more decisive and getting things done without the usual delays.

In what ways might you, or someone you know, be like Pamela? In what ways have you learned to sit on the fence rather than risk being criticized for your feelings, opinions or decisions? What critical people in your background made you feel you were better off acting unsure of yourself or not finishing things than to risk their disapproval for whatever you completed? As an adult, how are these habits of stopping, stalling, or avoiding commitments costing you more than you would like?

"Why Finish What I've Started When I Could Be More Excited About Something New Instead?"

The second overall reason for fencesitting has to do with the habit of stopping just prior to the completion of a project and, instead of working through the remaining obstacles, you lose interest and go off to start something new. It's as if we tell ourselves, "Why finish this difficult task when I could be starting something else that seems easy, at least at the beginning." Then when the next project gets difficult, you drop that one too, and start yet another.

Some people act this way in relationships—they drop each current partner when tensions arise and hope their new heartthrob will be easier. Others act this way in their work life—they abandon or procrastinate on projects that are nearing completion and instead get extremely excited and completely absorbed in the brainstorming stage of a new job or assignment that seems more glamorous, at least at the start.

Many people make the mistake of thinking the only way to have a fresh start is to walk out the door—to abandon a relationship or job in which you may have invested a lot of time and energy. That's not what I mean when I talk about getting off the fence and getting on with your life. Sometimes the more difficult but far more rewarding challenge is to make a decision and say, "I'm committed to this relationship and I'm going to work with my partner to make it better for both of us," or "I'm not done with this job yet and I'm going to make sure I resolve what's holding me back from completing what I've set out to accomplish."

For example, Jennifer is a woman in her mid-thirties who discovered that several of her closest friends and co-workers were going through divorces and career changes. All the upheavals among her peers made Jennifer ask herself, "What's wrong with me that I'm still in a marriage that has its ups and downs? Am I being lazy or holding myself back because I'm still on a career path that's slower than I once hoped?"

For several months, Jennifer kept fluctuating back and forth between thinking she should be initiating dramatic changes like everyone else. Half the time she was ready to break out and try something new. The other half had her wondering if it wasn't a better idea to hang in and make subtle improvements in her marriage and work situation.

Like many of us, Jennifer was tempted to drop everything and start from scratch in her love life and her work life. Yet when she discussed her marriage and her career with me in great detail, she recognized that each contained a lot that was worth keeping. Like many fencesitters, Jennifer's problem was not that she was in the wrong relationship or on the wrong career path. Rather, her problem was that she needed to stop thinking about leaving and start focusing instead on constructive ways to improve what could be improved and not change what was already working well.

Once Jennifer stopped fluctuating between, "Should I stay or should I go?," she began to initiate several minor changes that led to greater satisfaction and stability in both her marriage and her career. As I stated earlier, making a fresh start doesn't mean automatically walking out the door and starting over somewhere else. Quite often it means working through the unresolved issues that are close at hand in your love life, work life, family situation and personal goals.

"Sometimes It Feels Safer to Remain Stuck Than to Risk Taking the Next Step."

The third overall cause of fencesitting is that we often have good reasons—emotional baggage and fears from the past—to stall and stop on the way to a goal. Unless you identify and resolve those reasons for procrastinating you will find all sorts of good excuses for not following through on your goals. Remember, some of the biggest procrastinators are also the most intelligent and creative people. Your fears and hesitations are simply your mind's way of saying, "Hey, my friend, it's not safe to take the next step. Why not stall in the following creative ways . . ."

The trick is to calm your mind's fears and learn from your hesitations what needs to be watched for as you take the next step. It's counterproductive to ignore your fears or to be run by them. Yet by examining your hesitations and understanding your urge to procrastinate, you can identify what issues need to be resolved in order for you to take the next step forward.

Whenever you notice your mind is filled with doubts, fears, and excuses for not finishing a goal, you have two choices—you can let yourself procrastinate or you can catch yourself and learn what's going on inside your emotions so you can move forward safely and effectively. Instead of stuffing your fears inside or letting them disrupt your plans, I recommend you take a few moments to examine each hesitation and ask yourself these questions:

—Why am I hesitating? What fears of moving forward are making me indecisive or wanting to stall?

—What are my fears about? How might they be related more to a past experience or hurt from long ago than to the present situation?

—What can I learn from these insecurities? How can I

turn these fears into valuable clues of what I don't want to see happen again? How can I communicate my concerns to others so they will know what I expect and how not to hurt me?

—What can I do to make this time better than previous experiences? How can I learn from past mistakes and manage the current situation with more creativity and openness?

Instead of being shut down by your fears and hesitations, answering the above questions carefully will allow you to "Fear Forward," to keep making progress even though you have insecurities from past experiences which come to mind. To "Fear Forward" means to notice your fears, to learn from them, but not to be stopped or stalled by them. Instead of denying or disregarding your insecurities based on past experiences, you can use them for a source of insight and growth.

Some examples of what I mean by "Fear Forward" are:

—When you fall in love and yet realize your strong feelings for this person bring up fears from past hurts. Instead of stopping or stalling, this is a good time to talk about your fears and past experiences so that you can learn how to make sure they won't keep repeating themselves.

—When you feel overwhelmed by a difficult project at work or in raising your children. Instead of procrastinating, this is a good time to keep moving forward by asking others to give you support and assistance. Rather than feeling the entire burden is on your shoulders, use your fears to remind you that you need to ask for help.

—When you have a strong urge to take the next step in some area of your life but you find yourself stuck in indecision and uncertainty. Instead of beating yourself up with criticism, this is a good time to ask yourself what emotional baggage from the past is holding you up so you can resolve those issues and get on with your goals.

Sometimes right in the middle of feeling fearful and unsure of which direction to follow, you need to remind yourself of previous times in your life when you were persistent and your perseverance was successful. Looking back at prior times when you overcame your fears and took a risk, what do you recall of the following:

—Did you ever get rejected at first by someone you loved or a job you wanted, only to discover that through your persistence you were given a second chance?

—Were you ever told no several times when you proposed a new idea to someone at home or at work, only to find that they eventually said yes when you resubmitted your idea in a better form?

—Did you ever feel unsure of whether you could do something, but after focusing on that challenge for a long time you were finally triumphant?

There is a tremendous excitement that comes when you finally get off the fence and make a decision that can lead to greater happiness for you or someone you love. There is an unforgettable thrill when after several failures or setbacks your persistence pays off and you succeed at something which has eluded your grasp far too long.

When you find yourself stuck in a rut, remind yourself that you've been in ruts before and gotten out successfully. Only when you have a clear sense that you can actually succeed at your current challenge will you begin to develop creative ways to overcome the obstacles and make it happen.

What Will You Need to Let Go?

To break through a pattern of not making difficult decisions and not finishing important goals, you may need to give up some dearly held beliefs and habits. When I asked a group of "Recovering Fencesitters and Procrastinators" what they had to let go of in order to take the next step forward, here are some of the answers I received:

> I had to stop feeling sorry for myself. I'd become so used to falling short of a goal and then feeling sorry for myself that I felt awkward and unfamiliar with completing things and telling myself, "Way to go! You actually did it!

> I had to stop blaming other people for my habit of putting things off. It was so easy to blame my procrastination on other people's mistakes or other people's reluctance to help me out.

> I had to give up waiting for this illusion of the "perfect moment." I was always waiting for the right time when there would be no insecurities or uncertainties. Now I realize that moment may never come and meanwhile I can get on with my life even though I still have doubts and a little bit of second-guessing.

> I had to let go of my dependence on other people. I used to wait for others to push me along, coax me into doing things, and convince me to make the next move. Now I have to figure out what I want and motivate myself to do something about it. That's hard but it's also a relief to have control over my actions and decisions.

I had to stop worrying about failure and start seeing each decision or challenge as a chance to do something right, even if it didn't come out perfect. I still have moments when I think about what might go wrong, but I also remember to look at what might go right and that helps me take risks.

In your own life, what are the areas in which you are sitting on the fence, putting off a major decision or step forward? In each situation, it helps to find out not only what your goals are but also what you will need to give up in order to take the next step. What habits or patterns do you need to stop perpetuating? What fears and self-criticism do you need to resolve? What self-defeating attitudes do you need to work through in order to make a decision and follow through on your goals?

Here is a chance to take a brief inventory of your own procrastination/fencesitting profile. For each of the major areas of your life, think carefully about what might be holding you back and what you need to resolve in order to make improvements and increase your satisfaction.

—*In your primary relationship* . . .
What is the next step forward to make it better?
Why do you think you've been unable to take that next step thus far?
What self-defeating habit or attitude must you begin to resolve so that you can improve your primary relationship?

—*In your work life or household responsibilities* . . .
What is the next step forward to make it better?
Why do you think you've been unable to take that next step thus far?
What self-defeating habit or attitude must you begin to resolve so that you can improve your daily activities?

—*In your family situation* . . .
What is the next step forward to make it better?

Why do you think you've been unable to take that next step thus far?

What self-defeating habit or attitude must you begin to resolve so that you can improve your family situation?

—In your search for meaning and purpose . . .
What is the next step forward to make it stronger?

Why do you think you've been unable to take that next step thus far?

What self-limiting habit or attitude must you begin to resolve so that you can fully develop your spiritual search?

Please be careful when taking an inventory like this. You should be looking for insights of how to break out of old habits and develop a stronger momentum for moving forward. Asking these questions is *not* so you can beat yourself up and feel badly for what you haven't done. Rather, the time is right for asking questions that can help you uncover what's been holding you back and what is a more positive direction to follow.

Turning Ideas into Action

Now comes the most important step for anyone who suffers from a habit of stalling and stopping on the way to a cherished goal. You have some good ideas listed on the previous pages or in your mind about the next step you need to take. But will those good ideas lead to empty promises or satisfying accomplishments?

Every fencesitter or procrastinator has to face the fact that he or she is very talented at coming up with ways to stall and put off following through on a decision. Therefore, it's essential that you have on hand equally powerful ways to overcome those habits. You need special tools to prevent yourself from stalling and to renew your momentum when you feel gripped by indecision or sluggish from putting things off.

There are two extremely useful techniques you can employ whenever you notice the first signs that you are on the fence about a goal that means a great deal to you or someone you love. The first device is something I call "The Fencesitter's Method of Making Great Decisions." The second device is called "The Procrastinator's Trusty Guide to Following Through." Using either or both of these techniques could be threatening to your habit of sitting on the fence.

The Fencesitter's Method of Making Great Decisions

This technique can be used for major decisions such as getting married, having children, changing jobs, moving, etc., or less major but equally troubling decisions such as where to eat dinner, what to wear to an important event, what to give someone for a birthday present, or whether to sign up for an evening class.

If you have been a lifelong devotee of the art of fencesitting, you may feel offended that this method is so simple. Most people would rather ruminate, cogitate, and constipate about a decision for a long time. This technique may surprise you with its quickness, but that doesn't make it any less effective. Your goal is to make the best decision and by using this method you will do just that.

Here are the steps involved in coming to a great decision even when it seems impossible to make up your mind:

Step 1: Narrowing Your Options

The trouble with most fencesitters is that they like to

say, "On the other hand, and then on the other hand, and then on the other hand." How many hands do you have?

In this technique you are only allowed two options. They can be "Yes" and "No," or you can choose between two alternatives, which I'll call "A" or "B." You are not allowed to add "Maybe" or "C" or "A and maybe B."

Sometimes the key to making a good decision is to focus on two excellent options while eliminating all the options you know in your heart you would never choose. For example, Jay says he can't decide whether or not to get married. But if you press him to be more specific you'll find out that he's very much in love and knows he's going to want to get married sooner or later. He thought he was stuck with three options: A, to get married now; B, to get married a year or two from now; or C, not to get married at all. In fact, Jay's decision is much simpler. Since he's in love and knows he's going to want to get married eventually, he doesn't need to look at the option of "not getting married at all." He only has two options to choose between, A, to get married now; and B, to get married a year or two from now.

Focusing on a current decision or challenge for which you find yourself on the fence, take a moment to eliminate all the options except your two favorite choices. What are the two options that are most appealing to you to resolve this situation? Remember, you can only have two—a yes or no decision, or an A or B decision. Unlike the octopus, you can't keep saying, "On the other hand, on the other hand, on the other hand."

For your current "on the fence" dilemma, take a moment to describe your two *favorite* options. (You might want to write them down on a piece of paper.)

Step 2: Examining Your Excuses

Most people pretend they're serious about making a decision and then act surprised when delays and detours show up. To break the habit of fencesitting, you will need to be honest with yourself. What are your hidden reasons for wanting to put off this decision? What are your secret strategies for remaining on the fence?

Here are a few examples of common excuses people have for not wanting to make a decision. How many sound familiar?

> If I make up my mind, I'm bound to make someone angry.

> If I decide, I'll have to follow through and what if I find it's more difficult than I anticipated?

> If I get off the fence, I'll have to kiss goodbye the option I won't be selecting. I'd rather keep all my options alive and not have to settle for one.

> If I make a decision now and find out later I've made the wrong decision, will I have the good sense to change direction or be stuck with a bad decision?

> If I end my hesitation, it will mean I'm admitting to myself and to others what I really want. But what if I don't get what I want? Everyone will know I was vulnerable . . . and maybe it's better to pretend I don't really care.

Step 3: Examining Your Costs of Staying on the Fence

Once you've begun to consider your excuses or innermost fears of making a decision, then it's time to make a second list. This is your honest assessment of what you're losing and whom you're neglecting by staying on the fence. What are you giving up by not moving forward? What are you missing out on because of your indecision?

How is your fencesitting distracting you from other important goals and responsibilities? Who is your indecisiveness hurting or upsetting? What is your stalling costing you in terms of the trust others have in you or the trust you have for yourself?

Making this list of hidden costs allows you to face your stalling habit directly and honestly. Surely when you see what it's costing you, you begin to wonder if your excuses for delaying are as important as you once believed. When you look at what your fencesitting is forcing you to miss or whom your delay is hurting, you begin to feel motivated to stop resisting and finally make a decision.

Focusing on a decision or challenge for which you are currently on the fence, make a list of what your hesitation is costing you—emotionally, financially, interpersonally? After you've made your list of the "costs of stalling," read it over several times until you begin to feel just how important it is to break your hesitation and take the next step.

Here is an example of what can happen if you closely examine the costs of sitting on the fence too long:

Norma and Stuart have been married for seven years and have three children. Ever since they first met, they've talked about moving out of the city and starting a less high-pressure life in a different part of the country. Yet like many people who have trouble making decisions, they've held onto the fantasy of moving and not committed to the reality of actually moving. Norma admits, "It's much easier for us to fantasize all sorts of options of where we might move. If we actually moved, we'd probably have to deal with flaws and compromises that never enter into our fantasies."

Yet the indecision was costing them a great deal. When I asked them to make a list of the hidden costs of staying on the fence, they both wrote:

Arguments about when and where to move are causing a lot of friction in our relationship.

Both of us feel we don't want our children to grow up in this city. Not moving makes us feel we're letting our children down.

We keep putting off fixing up the place where we live because we don't know how long we'll be here. As a result, we're never comfortable or happy with our home.

We waste a lot of time talking to real estate agents and getting excited about places we then fail to commit to. This whole process of indecision is driving us crazy.

Only when they listed their costs, especially the one about not wanting their children to grow up in the city, did Norma and Stuart finally feel motivated to get off the fence and make a decision. While no decision would be "perfect," at last they could stop mulling it over and could get on with their lives.

Step 4: The Visualization Fantasy

Now you have a chance to see how creative and imaginative you are. In this step, you are to take your two options (Yes or No, A or B) and imagine each one of them coming true. HOWEVER, YOU DON'T NEED TO MAKE AN ACTUAL DECISION YET.

Start with your first option, the "Yes" or "A" decision. Close your eyes and imagine what it would be like if you chose this option, followed it through and could experience the results of your decision. What might it feel like in a few hours if you had chosen this first option? What will it be like in a week or a month if you chose "Yes" or "A"? What will happen over time, say in a year or five years, from your having chosen this first option? Let your imagination run wild and notice your feelings as you fantasize the good and not-so-good results that might occur from having chosen this first option.

Then relax for a moment and do it again for the second option. Close your eyes and imagine what it would be like if you chose "No" or "B." Follow it through and experience the results of your decision. What might it feel like in a few hours if you had chosen this second option? What will it be like in a week or a month if you chose "No" or "B"? What will happen over time, say in a year or five years, from your having chosen this second option? Let your imagination run wild and notice your feelings as you fantasize the good and not-so-good results that might occur from having chosen this second option.

Now open your eyes and relax for a moment. RE-MEMBER, IN THIS STEP YOU DON'T HAVE TO MAKE A DECISION YET. YOU ONLY NEED TO FANTASIZE THE FUTURE FROM HAVING CHO-SEN EACH OPTION.

Step 5: The Preference

Finally, you have reached the most interesting step. You will not be making a decision in the usual way you have done in the past. In this step you will be looking at your two options from a fresh and unique perspective.

Begin by taking a coin out of your pocket. A penny or nickel is fine, but if you want to get fancy about it you can use a half-dollar or a silver dollar.

Now here are the rules. If the coin were flipped and it landed on heads you would be forced to choose "Yes" or "A." If the coin were flipped and it landed on tails you would be forced to choose "No" or "B."

Without flipping the coin, close your eyes and ask yourself this simple question, "Which way do I want the coin to land? Heads mean 'Yes' or 'A.' Tails mean 'No' or 'B.' Which way do I really wish it would land?"

When you open your eyes, state out loud whether you

chose heads or tails. Which way did you really wish it would land? (Remember that the coin has to land on one or the other side. It can never land on both or the edge.)

Believe it or not, you have made a decision. The secret now is to make sure you don't go back on your feelings and pretend they weren't true. The reason this is the best decision for you is because it comes closest to your actual desires.

Here's how this technique went around your usual resistance to making a decision: When you visualized both options, you didn't have to inhibit yourself with the idea that you were about to make a decision. By not having to decide yet, you were free to explore your true feelings. Then you weren't asked to make a decision but to admit what your innermost desire was—heads or tails. That went around your reluctance to decide and focused directly on your best decision. Now it's time to follow through and make it happen.

Using this technique, I have found repeatedly that people who insisted they couldn't make up their minds were somehow able to get in touch with their innermost desires and admit them when they were asked, "Which way do I really wish the coin would land?" That's the moment in which the truth comes out, in which the cogitating and constipating gives way to a simple statement of your preference. It might not be the perfect decision, but it's your best chance to get off the fence and get on with your life.

"The Toughest Decision I've Ever Made"

Gina's case illustrates the struggle to make a difficult decision and the usefulness of the technique described above. An unmarried woman in her late thirties, Gina has known for years that she wanted to have a child yet has never been able to find the right partner for a long-term relationship. Now she feels close to the limit of her biological clock. According to Gina, "This is the toughest decision I've ever made. Do I choose to have a child or keep putting it off until maybe it's too late?"

Most of the time when Gina sat down to make a decision she found herself overwhelmed by unresolved issues and unanswerable questions. Could she be happy if she adopted a child later on? What if she got into a relationship with someone who had children already—would that satisfy her desire to raise children? What if she sublimated her need to be a parent by instead becoming more involved in activities that helped young children?

Or if she did decide to have a baby, how would she manage financially? How would she find time for everything? How would she explain her decision to the child later on? How would she deal with society's values and her family's reactions? Would it solve her problem or simply create newer and tougher problems?

When I asked Gina to use the exercise described earlier, her initial reaction was hesitation. She admitted, "I'm not sure I want some technique that is going to get me to make a decision." Yet when she thought it over, she realized she was moving dangerously close to the time when the decision would no longer be hers to make. Once she reached a certain age, the choice of having a child of her own might no longer be possible. Gina wanted to make up her mind before she lost the freedom to choose.

Visualizing her two options—to wait or to get pregnant—caused a variety of strong feelings for Gina. She describes, "When I thought about waiting, I tried to talk myself into being happy about adopting or living with someone else's children. While there's nothing wrong with those options, I realized my strong inner sense told me that isn't what I want. The more I tried to imagine being satisfied without having experienced childbirth, the more I began to sense a strong preference to go through with it."

Then when Gina visualized having a child, something interesting occurred. She explains, "I had always felt cloudy and indecisive because I'd fluctuated back and forth between the two options. But when I was asked to imagine what might happen if I chose this one—to actually have a child—I felt a renewed sense of inner strength and resolve that, no matter what, I could deal with the complexities."

She continues, "I realized I would find a way to pay the bills, handle the conflicting demands on my time, and deal with what other people thought of a single parent. Instead of feeling cloudy or unsure, I saw myself doing it and feeling committed to making sure I did the best I could."

Like many people who had been stuck on the fence for a long time, Gina could no longer lie to herself that she didn't have a strong preference. When she was asked, "Which way do you really wish the coin would land—heads to wait or tails to get pregnant," she knew exactly which she wanted. Gina's normally quiet, unsure tone gave way to a clear answer. "I want to have a child," she said. "I've never felt so sure about anything in my whole life."

Certainly there were many remaining issues that needed to be addressed—who would be the father, what role he should play in the child's upbringing, how Gina would deal with finances, child care, society, and her family. Yet for the first time in years, Gina knew what course of action she needed to take. Her struggle was no longer to make up her mind but to carry out what was probably the most important decision of her life. As she describes, "I know I haven't made the 'perfect' decision or the 'easy' choice. But I've finally gotten to what I really desire and I'm going to make sure I don't stop short of doing the best job possible. I can see myself in fifteen or twenty years telling my child how important this decision was and how glad I am to have felt this strongly about bringing a new life into this world."

The Procrastinator's Trusty Guide to Following Through

In many instances, once you have made a decision, *then* the difficult part begins. Following through on even the most heartfelt choices is not easy for many people. This next technique can be used whenever you find yourself stalling, delaying, or getting distracted from completing an important goal. You don't need to berate yourself with criticism for your habit of stopping or finding detours. Rather, you need to use the following device for refocusing your efforts. Here's what you can do to break out of procrastination and get on with a task or activity that needs to be completed:

Step 1: Have a Sense of Humor About Your Distractions

Instead of feeling as though you're a terrible person because you keep putting off an important task, lighten up a bit. Enjoy the brilliance of your stalling mind. What incredible excuses did you come up with this time not to focus and complete your work? What amazing interruptions and diversions were created just in time to keep you from finishing what you started?

Here are a few examples from some of the most ingenious procrastinators I've known:

> I have an uncanny talent for getting sick right when I'm about to finish something or present it to others. It's a very special talent to be able to get the flu or bronchitis

or something worse just when it looks like I'm going to break tradition and finish something on time. How do I do it? It's an old family secret. If you have to ask, then it's clear you don't have the talent anyway.

My most brilliant tactic for not completing things is always to work on three projects at once. The minute it looks like I'm making progress on one, I find myself distracted and thinking about another. It works every time; I never complete anything because I'm always jumping from one unfinished project to the other.

I'm so creative with procrastination that I don't even have to invent delays of my own—my husband and my kids always find a way to interrupt whatever I'm trying to accomplish or finish. The minute I sit down to complete one of my projects, my husband calls in a panic with some emergency that I need to drive his elderly mother somewhere, or that I need to get things ready for an important dinner guest from out of town. Or my kids come home from school with bleeding knees or a high fever and my glorious time to finish a project is gone.

My greatest procrastination device is so simple and so common, yet it works so well. All I have to do is interrupt my work and answer the phone when it rings. People tell me to get an answering machine and screen calls, but that would be so unlike me. My habit is that right in the middle of focusing on an important task, I pick up the phone and wind up in a conversation that goes on and on. Then by the time I get off the phone, I've lost my concentration and my work gets put off again.

Notice in each case that you can admit what you do to procrastinate without considering yourself a bad person. You simply need to tell the truth about the distractions and delays that keep you from finishing things. Only when you see the humor in your habit can you begin to change it.

Step 2: What Am I Trying to Avoid by Not Finishing This?

Even if you have great intentions to complete a task and not procrastinate, there may be strong emotional reasons why your mind is filled with distractions. Quite often the only way to stop procrastinating and get back on track is to uncover what those emotional obstacles might be.

The simplest way to find out what is holding you back from completing something is to ask yourself: "What am I trying to avoid by not finishing this?"

In most cases your answer will consist of one or more of the following:

—*Not finishing allows you to avoid getting criticized.* For example, if you don't complete a book, a report, an art project, or a redecorating effort, no one can criticize your work. You can continue to say, "It's not ready yet. I'm still working on it."

—*Not finishing allows you to postpone having to go onto the next phase, which might be even more difficult.* For example, if you are reluctant to look for a new job, the best way to procrastinate is to have trouble finishing your resume. The longer you stall and say your resume isn't right yet, the longer you can put off the more challenging task of interviewing for a job, choosing the one that suits you best, and starting out in a new assignment.

—*Not finishing allows you to avoid having to be responsible.* As long as you stall and delay, you can keep blaming your procrastination on other people. If you finished the project, you'd be forced to admit, "This is what I've accomplished . . . this is who I am." For many people, it's safer to keep your talents and ideas hidden than to face the responsibility of saying, "This is what I'm committed to . . . this is what I stand for."

Looking at a goal or project for which you are currently procrastinating, ask yourself: "What am I trying to avoid by not finishing this?" "What risk am I afraid to take and as a result I'm stalling and finding distractions?"

Without putting yourself down, what do you think is the honest reason why you are holding yourself back in this situation?

Facing your fear of moving forward is the key to breaking a lifelong habit of procrastination. When you take a moment to look within at what you are trying to avoid, you regain control over your situation. Instead of being surprised at the delay tactics that come up when you attempt to finish a task, you will recognize what's holding you back.

At this point, you need to talk over your doubts and fears of moving forward with someone (a friend, counselor, or support group) who can listen and understand your concerns. Only when you have addressed your emotional baggage will you be free to complete this goal and not be held back again and again.

Step 3: What Payoffs Will I Receive If I Complete This Project?

Now is the time to move beyond your fears and start making the task of completing things more enjoyable. No matter what goal you are trying to finish, the key to doing it well is to reward yourself at frequent intervals for every small step forward. Unless you treat yourself with respect and encouragement at every stage of growth, you will feel tempted again to stall, quit, or get involved in distractions.

For example, let's say you are procrastinating over whether or not to lose weight. You promise yourself on the scale that you're going to lose ten pounds but then when it's late at night and there are goodies in the refrigerator all promises are called off.

The mistake most people make when they are dieting is to focus only on what the scale reveals about your weight and to neglect to reward yourself for all the small steps forward you might be taking to improve your diet, health, and energy level. Instead of criticizing yourself for not losing ten pounds quickly, you need to acknowledge yourself for every new behavior you do that points in the right direction. If you say no to a fattening dessert, that entitles you to be rewarded with a relaxing bubble bath. If you spend twenty minutes a day doing exercises or taking a brisk walk, that entitles you to be rewarded with a new record album or cassette. If you replace fattening snacks with tasty vegetable treats and lots of water, that entitles you to be rewarded with a trip to the movies or a museum.

The secret for breaking out of procrastination and enjoying the process of completing your goals is to break each challenge up into small, manageable steps and give yourself a satisfying reward for each step you accomplish. Pretty soon you will be focused not on the unattained final goal but on your success at achieving each small step along the way.

To apply this technique to your own procrastination habits, think about a current project or goal about which you have been stalling. Instead of focusing only on the final step of the project, break it up into several small steps that can be accomplished in a short amount of time. Then promise yourself a satisfying reward for each small step accomplished. Instead of feeling as though you are climbing a steep hill, you will once again feel as though you are engaging in a pleasurable journey. Rather than thinking you are miles from your goal, you will find yourself being rewarded frequently for small successes on the way to a desired outcome.

One way to create an easier route to a goal for which you have been procrastinating is to make a "Small Step,

Big Reward" Chart. Write down the first positive new behavior you should do to move toward your goal. Then write down a reward you will get for completing that first step. Then write down a second small accomplishment that could improve your odds of reaching your desired outcome, along with a reward if you complete that small step. And so on, until you have broken your goal up into five to ten manageable steps that will be a lot easier to achieve than looking at the whole task at once. Remember, however, that you must reward yourself for each small step. If you fail to keep your promise and you don't get rewarded for your tiny steps forward, pretty soon you'll stop or stall again.

I've used this technique in writing this book. When I thought about writing eight chapters and covering hundreds of topics, the feeling was overwhelming. Even to sit down and try to write a single chapter felt like an ordeal. So to write this book I broke each chapter up into dozens of small steps. One step was to outline the chapter, after which I gave myself a reward. The next step was to try out several different opening paragraphs, after which I gave myself a satisfying treat. The next step was to write a few pages a day on a specific topic from the chapter outline, after which I made sure to take a break and give myself a payoff. Eventually, one step at a time, I would complete each chapter and be sure to make a special occasion out of each small completion. Only by focusing on small steps and satisfying incentives was I able to avoid the procrastination and delays that can so easily plague someone writing a sizable manuscript.

I hope you will use a similar approach whenever you find yourself feeling overwhelmed by a difficult or lengthy task. There's nothing wrong with holding incentives in front of yourself to make sure you get the job done. With creative and humorous incentives to look forward to, you will find that instead of feeling like an ordeal your major goals will begin to feel like an enjoyable adventure.

Step 4: The Weekly Boost of Support

In addition to the goals and payoffs you give to yourself, you may also need the support of other people in order to stay focused on your task and not fall back into procrastination. One technique that has been successful for many people is to have a friend, relative or colleague be your "antiprocrastination partner" as you proceed through a difficult project. Here's how it works:

1. Choose someone who also is going through a difficult challenge. Together you can support each other without either antiprocrastination partner feeling better or smaller than the other.

2. At least once a week, you and your antiprocrastination partner should meet for lunch or set aside a special time for a lengthy phone call. During that lunch or phone conversation you are to take turns describing all the obstacles and delays that came up during the past several days and how you overcame or were stopped by those delays. First, one person describes how he or she is doing in sticking to the goals that were discussed the week before. Then the other person describes his or her progress and setbacks. You will notice that both of you have had obstacles to face, yet both of you have continued to press on toward your goals. Even if there have been delays, the fact that you are both still moving forward will provide an added boost of support for each of you.

3. Finally, after giving each other support and encouragement, you should take turns at the end of the lunch or phone call to discuss your goals for the upcoming week. Make sure your goals are realistic and that you've broken up your tasks into small, manageable steps with a reward planned for each small accomplishment. You and your antiprocrastination partner are there for each other to remind one another of the small steps you need to take and the satisfying rewards you have promised yourselves.

With the support of your antiprocrastination partner, you will have added motivation to stick to your goals and follow through with even the most challenging tasks.

To overcome a habit of fencesitting and procrastination is not always simple or direct. Sometimes you may find yourself falling back into old habits of stopping or stalling even when there are good reasons to move forward. Yet if you use the techniques described on the preceding pages, you may be able to catch yourself and not give in to the desire to procrastinate. Perhaps one day you will use these exercises to revise the Scarlett O'Hara line and say instead, "I'll think of it today. I don't need to wait until tomorrow."

How to Keep Other People from Dumping Their Baggage on You

8

> No one can make you feel inferior
> without your consent.
> —Eleanor Roosevelt

A few months ago, in the middle of working on this book and several other projects, I received an assignment to write an article for a major national magazine. The editor and I agreed about the topics that would be included. From our initial phone call, I thought this assignment was going to be a breeze.

Then four weeks later I handed in the first draft. Suddenly the editor changed from a supportive ally into a condescending critic. In a sarcastic tone, he said he no longer wanted the article. He didn't want a rewrite—in fact, he claimed he never should have assigned the piece in the first place. Then without waiting for a reply from me, he hung up.

When I got off the phone, I felt like I'd been hit by a truck. That day I was scheduled to rewrite a chapter for this book and give a one-hour radio interview over the telephone with a New England station. At that moment, however, I couldn't imagine doing anything productive. I felt confused and hurt. Why had this editor been so rude and condescending? How could I think clearly or give a radio interview with this incident on my mind? I called the editor back, but his secretary said he'd left for lunch.

For the next few minutes I felt almost like a scolded child who had done something terrible. Even though I enjoy writing and have been successful as an author, getting rejected is never easy. My mind was filled with self-doubts and uncertainties.

In the middle of feeling unsure of myself, I stopped and remembered the famous quote from Eleanor Roosevelt—"No one can make you feel inferior without your consent." Thinking about what she meant by that, I realized I had a choice to make. I could either let this editor's condescension shut me down and cause me to spend a lot of energy feeling sorry for myself and resenting him. Or I could heal my wounds, learn something constructive from this experience, and get on with my life.

Once I realized I had a choice in the matter, I began to look at the rejection differently. Yes, the editor had unloaded some belittling comments in my lap. But how much of it had to do with me personally? Maybe he was having a bad day. Possibly his editor-in-chief had vetoed the idea and this editor was covering up for his boss. Maybe there were some things I could learn from his criticism about improving my writing skills or negotiating clearer guidelines with busy editors. Possibly I hadn't given this article enough time or energy. But did any of these mean I should feel like a worthless nothing and beat myself up with criticism?

I spent the next half hour using some of the "Letting Go" exercises described in Chapter Two of this book to get this editor's condescension out of my system and to regain my sense of focus and well-being. By the time I went back to work a short time later, I felt renewed and ready to do an even better job than if this incident hadn't taken place. I also made a vow to myself to make sure the next time I got an article assignment, the editor and I would work closely together to avoid miscommunications and faulty assumptions. That way I might be able to prevent a repetition of what had thrown me off center that morning.

In your own work environment and personal life, how do you deal with situations that are similar to the one described above? How do you cope with rejection, criticism, and belittling comments? When someone at work, at home, or in your family is having a bad day and this person takes it out on you, how do you heal your wounds and regain your sense of self-worth?

This chapter is about following through on the goals you've set for yourself throughout this book. Yet in order to achieve these changes and improvements in your life, you will need to make sure your fresh starts aren't thwarted by critical individuals who knowingly or unknowingly want to keep you in your place. In the pages that follow, you will learn how to recognize when someone is trying to hold you back or keep their power over you—and, most importantly, what you can do about it. You will also discover when you might be holding yourself back, and you will be given creative ways to overcome several forms of self-sabotage.

Innocent Bystanders

Have you ever started your day in a great mood and then gotten clobbered by someone else's complaints, criticism or attempts to make you feel small? Have you ever set an important goal for yourself and then found it was extremely difficult to achieve because of the resistance you got from other people?

There are some psychologists who will tell you there is no such thing as opposition to your plans—that if you think positive thoughts no one will do anything against you. While this type of optimism might be enticing, it isn't accurate. In everyday life you and I clearly encounter situations in which people take out their frustrations on innocent bystanders or criticize those they cannot understand or accept.

Sometimes it's because you are in the wrong place at the wrong time—your boss, your romantic partner, or a family member takes a small thing you did and turns it into an opportunity to unload a huge backlog of anger that has more to do with other people than with you. Other times it's because someone has some valuable feedback to give you, but unfortunately he or she throws in a host of attacks and criticisms as well. If only people could express their opinions without resorting to personal attacks or attempts to dominate and control.

Still other times people might ventilate their anger and frustrations at us simply because we are the only ones who will listen. You might have a boss, spouse, relative, or friend who has few outlets for her or his dissatisfactions. Taking advantage of your kindness, this person might unknowingly be using you as a garbage dump for her or his complaints.

If you live with, work with, or are related to someone who is in the habit of giving out condescending remarks or merciless criticism, it can take a toll on your health and sense of self-worth. You can talk about making a fresh start until you are blue in the face, but until you learn how to deal with the people in your daily life who are dumping their emotional baggage on you, it's not likely much progress will be made.

Many of us try to be "nice" and "understanding" in our business, personal, and family relationships. While there's nothing wrong with being a nice person, there is something wrong with letting other people take their aggressions out on you. If you truly respect yourself and are sincere about the steps forward you want to make in your life, including your plans to be of service to others, you first need to learn creative ways to deal with people whose conscious or unconscious plan is to belittle, dominate or control you. You owe it to yourself and those you love to start learning how to stand up for yourself in difficult situations.

Those Who Would Try to Make You Feel Small

While there are many different ways people tend to dump their anger and hurts in the laps of unsuspecting lovers and co-workers, there are three especially common varieties that most of us have to deal with frequently. I call these three kinds of people: "The Person Who Needs to Be Right," "The Person Who Likes to Blame," and "The Person Who Loves to Find Something to Pick At." Most of us are either living with, working with, or related to someone who fits these descriptions at least some of the time. In some cases, we need to look at how we ourselves exhibit these belittling behaviors.

See how many of the following characteristics ring true about yourself or someone you know:

"The Person Who Needs to Be Right" . . .

—likes to win every argument even if this person isn't completely sure of what he or she is saying.

—doesn't believe there are two sides to every issue— thinks instead there is one way, the "right way."

—tends not to listen while the other person is talking— instead he or she is planning a comeback line or getting ready to interrupt and launch a counterattack.

—as a child, this person grew up always feeling criticized, belittled, or unable to win an argument in his or her family.

—as an adult, this person has seemed to win many arguments in the short run, but in the long run he or she has lost jobs, friends, and relationships because no one will put up with that kind of bullying and stubbornness for too long.

Whom does this description sound like? Your boss, your romantic partner, a family member, a close friend, yourself? When in the past few weeks or months have you locked horns in battle with someone who desperately needs to be right and tries to make everyone else feel small in order that he or she might feel big even for a moment? How well did you handle the situation—did this person squash and belittle you, or did you find a way to hold onto your self-esteem and take good care of yourself?

Before we deal with solutions, let's look at another kind of difficult person—the one who likes to blame.

"The Person Who Likes to Blame" . . .

—always can find someone or something else to hold responsible for the mistakes or oversights this person refuses to admit about himself or herself.

—doesn't feel comfortable looking at his or her own contribution to a problem—thinks instead that if only others would change, everything would be fine.

—tends not to listen when the other person is pointing out the obvious ways both sides brought on the problem—instead he or she is planning a guilt-inducing ploy to make the other person feel responsible.

—as a child, this person grew up always feeling blamed, unappreciated, and criticized, even for things he or she didn't do.

—as an adult, this person has been successful on several occasions in making others feel guilty and has escaped criticism in the short run, but in the long run he or she has lost friends, jobs, and relationships because no one will put up with that kind of defensiveness and attacking for too long.

Who is the blamer in your life that fits this description? Is it someone you live with, work with or grew up with? Is it you? When was the last time a blamer stubbornly accused you of something in order to protect his or her own ego? What can you do besides engaging in an endless argument that goes nowhere?

There is one more description we need to look at before discussing possible ways to regain your sanity when confronted by people like this. The third character type is called "The Person Who Loves to Find Something to Pick At." Just from the title alone, who comes to mind as someone who has an incredible knack for always complaining about something?

"The Person Who Loves to Find Something to Pick At" . . .

—always can find something to criticize about what you did no matter how well you did it.

—doesn't feel comfortable giving out too much praise or credit because he or she thinks it will make people lazy, conceited, or less motivated to jump when this person says "Jump."

—tends to be equally or even more critical of his or her own performance. This person never is satisfied with even the most remarkable things.

—as a child, this person grew up always feeling judged, pushed, and unappreciated, forever being told "You aren't doing enough," "That's not good enough" or "We expect so much more from you."

—as an adult, this person has been successful at times

in getting others to try extra hard to meet his or her unrealistically high expectations, but sooner or later this person loses jobs and relationships because no one can put up with that much criticism for too long.

As you think about the three kinds of people described above, notice that each of them tries to make other people feel small because he or she felt criticized and belittled while growing up. Their difficult behavior is not something that can change overnight. It comes from deep feelings of inadequacy and self-criticism that unfortunately are projected out on innocent bystanders like you. People who need to be right all the time, who blame others for their own mistakes, or who attack you with unnecessary criticism are individuals who barely know the pattern they have fallen into. From their point of view, they feel justified in being so self-righteous and condescending. They usually don't realize the price they are paying from treating others with such disrespect.

How to Deal With Critical and Controlling People

If someone repeatedly tries to attack your good ideas for making progress in your life, what can you do to prevent their negativity from undermining your efforts? Or if someone tries to belittle the hard work you've done and the growth you've made recently, how do you make sure *their* doubts and worries don't become *your* doubts and worries?

To deal effectively with someone in your life who is extremely critical or controlling, there are two options you can use. Some people use only one of the following, while others use both options to cope with a difficult boss, spouse, relative, co-worker, or friend. The next time someone is attempting to belittle your ideas or undermine your efforts to do something constructive, try the following:

Option 1:
Make Sure You Separate This Person's Anxieties from Your Own Self-Worth and Steps Forward.

If you live with, work with, or are related to someone who tends to find fault with whatever positive steps you take in your life, it's very important that you recognize you are dealing with someone who has a problem that doesn't need to become your problem. This critical person probably grew up being criticized and, as an adult, this individual is even harsher on himself or herself than on you.

The most intelligent thing you can do whenever this person is belittling you, blaming you, or picking at something you did is to stop, relax and remind yourself, "I don't need to accept this person's criticism if it's not accurate. No one can make me feel inferior without my consent."

That may not sound like much, but it can be a very powerful technique, especially if you remember to use it right at the moment when this person is dumping anger or condescension on you. For example, I have seen women and men with extremely critical bosses use this technique to regain their self-esteem and not be squashed by their boss's harsh criticism. I have seen wives and husbands avoid being controlled or held back by their spouse simply by remembering, "I don't need to accept this person's criticism if it's not accurate. No one can make me feel inferior without my consent." I've also seen women and men stand up to critical parents and other relatives by remembering these lines. Recall these words right at the moment when someone is trying to make you feel guilty and do things their way instead of the way you know is right for you.

If someone has doubts and worries about the positive steps you are making in your life, you can listen respectfully and take whatever is valuable in their advice *without* accepting the belittling remarks or inaccurate judgments that have been thrown in as well. For example, when Alison, a twenty-eight-year-old stock analyst, decided to take a year off from work and do some traveling, everyone gave her a hard time. Her family thought she was being selfish. Her co-workers thought she was ruining her chances for advancement. Her lover was angry that she had the nerve to think she could get along without him. Alison's best friend warned her, "You could be losing a great job and a great guy if you do this."

According to Alison, "If I had taken to heart all of the criticism and worries people tried to lay on me, I never would have gone. I didn't mind that people had opinions or suggested things I needed to consider. What I couldn't stand was how much they tried to make their fears into my fears. No one just gave me a suggestion and said, 'That's for you to consider—do whatever you decide is best.' Instead, they each seemed to be saying it was selfish or irresponsible to go."

Once Alison removed herself from the anxiety-producing comments of her parents, her co-workers, her lover, and her best friend, she tried to regain her own sense of what were the pros and cons of taking a year off to travel. As Alison recalls, "I wasn't doing it to be irresponsible or to jeopardize my career or my relationship. I was doing it because I knew that taking a year off was going to benefit my health and add to what I might offer others in my career and my personal life. Once I stopped letting other people's fears make me want to give up my plans, I remembered how much I needed to take this opportunity to grow while I still had the time and the flexibility to do it."

Choosing to follow her own instincts rather than the warnings of those around her, Alison made arrangements to spend a year in Europe and the Far East. At first she had doubts about her decision and wondered if everyone else's fears had been correct. But after several months of traveling and visiting different countries, Alison no longer regretted her adventurous choice. When she came back to the United States, she not only had gained a stronger sense of her potential but also found that her increased knowledge of international business had qualified her to make an important career move.

While not all of us can afford to travel for a year, we each have areas of our lives in which we possess adventurous ideas that those around us tend to criticize. If we let other people's fears and anxieties hold us back, we may win their agreement but lose our own chance to develop into fuller human beings. Sometimes we need to get beyond the fear of losing a relationship in order to take that relationship to the next level of growth. Sometimes we need to let go of our fear of losing a job in order to turn that job into something more stimulating and fulfilling. Sometimes we need to risk doing something from the heart, for ourselves or for other people, in order to find out what we are capable of accomplishing during the short time we have on Earth.

Option 2:
You Need to Teach the Overly Critical People in Your Life What You Will No Longer Tolerate and How You Would Like to Be Treated.

While you shouldn't expect to change a fault-finding person overnight, you can set firm limits that force this person to change the way he or she treats you in specific situations. Even if it feels easier to avoid this person altogether, there are tremendous possible benefits that can be achieved when you constructively teach this person what you find hard to take about his or her criticism and what you would prefer instead.

If you spend your entire life running away from people and situations that are critical or demanding of you, you may never develop the important skills of learning to stand up for yourself in a loving and effective way. Too often people are forced to quit a job or end a relationship because they don't know how to deal with a critical person at work or at home. While in some cases it is appropriate to leave an abusive situation in which a dictatorial or alcoholic boss or spouse constantly threatens your well-being, in many cases you can improve a difficult work or love relationship simply by learning how to teach the other person what you will no longer tolerate and how you would like to be treated.

For example, Jay is a computer programmer who has an extremely critical boss. Tense and overworked, Jay's boss tends to blow up everytime he finds a small mistake in Jay's work. While Jay has thought about quitting, he isn't ready to sacrifice all the years he devoted to this company. As Jay described, "I like most of the people I work with here. My boss is the only hard case. Besides, I would hate to give up this position because after years of low-level jobs I've finally been promoted to something that really challenges me professionally."

Instead of quitting, Jay decided to stand up to his boss in a way that wouldn't threaten him or get Jay fired. First, Jay began to practice separating his boss' temper tantrums from Jay's own sense of self-worth and competence. Every time his boss breathed down Jay's neck or exploded because of a small mistake, Jay remembered to tell himself, "No one can make you feel inferior without your consent."

In addition, Jay began to teach his boss in a nonthreatening way what Jay needed in order for them to work together. During the rare moments when Jay noticed his boss was relaxed or in a good mood, he began planting suggestions in his mind. Several times Jay commented to his boss in a direct but nonaccusatory way, "I've been thinking about how to improve the efficiency around here and I've got an idea on how you can get better work out of me. I tend to get nervous and make a lot of mistakes when someone is watching me too closely. So if we could set up a system where I do my work on my own most of the time and then bring you my projects for feedback every few days, that would help me make fewer mistakes."

Jay also suggested to his boss, "I was reading a book the other day and I heard about something called a 'feedback sandwich.' The best way to give criticism is to start out by offering a few things you like, then a few things that could be improved, and finally a supportive comment about how you have confidence in this person making the changes that need to be made. I think if you used the feedback sandwich technique on me, it would help me understand what you need a lot quicker than if you just tell me what I'm doing wrong. I'm going to use it with the people I supervise and I'd love it if you'd try it out when you're giving me feedback."

Notice that Jay didn't attack, criticize, or accuse his boss of anything. Instead he explained in a gentle way what he needed, what tended to make him nervous and inefficient, and what could be improved. Even though it took several explanations before his boss fully understood and started using these suggestions, eventually Jay discovered some noticeable improvements at work. He describes, "My boss was resistant at first but then he really got into this 'feedback sandwich' idea. Not only does it soften the blow of his criticism, but it makes me feel good that I actually taught this anxious wreck how to treat me and the others in my department with a little more respect."

Marianne used a similar technique to improve her relationship with an overly critical husband. Even though Marianne is quite attractive, her husband had fallen into the habit of making negative comments about her weight and the fact that her figure was no longer what it had been twenty years ago when they first got married.

At first Marianne fluctuated between keeping her feelings silent or exploding with her own insults about her husband's expanding jelly roll. When I suggested she could teach her husband what she wouldn't tolerate and how she would like to be treated, Marianne wasn't interested. She commented, "I don't have the patience to teach him anything. What I'd rather do is make him feel as insecure about the way he looks as he makes me feel about myself."

Then one night after Marianne and her husband were attempting to celebrate their anniversary and instead got into a nasty fight about how critical they are of each other, she decided it was time to try something new. She resolved to stop using sarcastic comebacks and start admitting how she really felt about her husband's comments about her figure.

With tears in her eyes, Marianne described to her husband how hard it was for her to feel good about their marriage or enjoy being with him when she had to listen to his constant remarks about her weight. She explained, "I love you very much and I want us to be close. But I have too much self-respect to stay in a relationship with someone who tries to belittle me or make me feel bad about the way I look. The reason I don't look like I did twenty years ago is not because I'm lazy or I don't love you. It's because I've given us three kids that bring us a lot of joy. It's because I've grown into a mature woman who needs your respect and your companionship, not your teasing or sarcasm. I love you and I hope you can find a way to appreciate me the way I am now, just as I need to appreciate you the way you are now."

By explaining to her husband exactly how she felt and why it was no longer acceptable for him to make fun of her figure, Marianne had taken an enormous risk. But when someone you love, especially a spouse, lover, brother, sister, or parent is hurting you with their fault-finding or criticism, you need to risk appearing vulnerable in order to let them know they don't have the right to talk to you that way. Fortunately, in Marianne's case as in so many others, her husband saw that she was standing up for herself out of self-respect and out of love for him and their relationship. Even though he didn't change overnight, gradually he learned to stop making critical remarks that were harmful to his wife and damaging to their marriage.

When dealing with people who always need to be right, who blame others for their own mistakes or who love to find fault, there is no guarantee that your efforts to teach them how you would like to be treated will be successful. In some cases, you may need to take a vacation from their critical comments or end your dealings with them altogether if they insist on being verbally or physically abusive.

What's most important is that you don't forget the rights and responsibilities you have in any romantic, work, or family relationship. Even if you are dealing with judgmental or critical individuals, no one can take away from you the following.

—*You have the right to be different.* Even if you are surrounded by people who think the whole world should be just like they are, you still have the right to be exactly who you are and not have to apologize for not being like them.

—*You have the right to disagree.* When you and someone you love have differing points of view, remind that person you still love them even though the two of you should agree to disagree on this particular issue. It's not disrespectful or unloving to say to a spouse, parent, brother, sister, or child, "I understand how you feel the way you do, and I need you to understand why I feel the way I feel." When two people love each other enough to allow for their differences and respective points of view, then their marriage, partnership, friendship, or family relationship has the potential to grow and survive even the most challenging disagreements.

—*You have the right to your feelings.* Too often people will tell you, "Don't be so sensitive," "You shouldn't feel that way," or "What are you making such a big deal about?" You have every right to be sensitive and to use your sensitivity to let others know how to treat you with respect. You have every right to feel the way you do about things that matter to you, even if they don't matter as much to those around you. You have every right to stand up for issues that feel important to you, even if those important concerns aren't in vogue with those who would rather you kept silent.

What If Others Are Threatened by the Changes You Make?

Imagine for a moment that you've finished reading this book at least once and you are beginning to apply some of the insights and exercises to your own life. You are putting into practice the ideas and skills you've acquired about how to improve your relationships, your work life, your family situation, your sense of meaning and purpose, and your procrastination.

Suddenly and without warning, you encounter some

stiff opposition. Someone with strong opinions tries to convince you that your goals are unrealistic, that your ideas are naïve, or that your efforts are futile. Someone close to you, whom you thought would support the changes you are starting to make, instead feels threatened and tries to keep things the way they were. Someone you live with or work with attempts to reestablish their power over you and, in the process, this person tries to make you feel guilty or small so that he or she can feel strong and superior.

At this point, you will have to make a choice. You can either let the opposition you face shut you down and force you to go back to the dissatisfying way things were. Or you can find out why this person is dumping his or her emotional baggage in your lap; then, instead of shutting down, you can stick to your vision of how things could be improved.

One of the toughest challenges of carrying out your goals from this book might be the resistance you get from other people. Relatives and friends, who have gotten used to the way you were before, may feel threatened by the changes they see in you now. Those who have come to rely on you for your willingness to do things *their way* might resent your efforts to find a way that works better for you. Anyone who has enjoyed feeling above you in an area in which you were struggling may now feel bitter that you are passing them by.

To give you an idea of some of the potential roadblocks and issues you may face as you make improvements in your life, consider the following:

1. If you were developing exactly the kind of relationship you desire most, who would be resistant or upset?

   —your current partner   —a good friend
   —an ex-spouse or lover   —your children

          —a parent or relative   —a co-worker
          —a brother or sister   —who else?

  2. If you arranged exactly the kind of work situation
     and income you desire most, who would be jealous
     or critical?

  3. If you initiated exactly the kind of family get-togethers
     you desire most, who would be threatened or difficult?

  4. If you have exactly the kind of spiritual or religious
     life you desire most, who would be offended or
     angry?

Ironically, some of the most troublesome criticisms
and impediments may come from those you love dearly.
For example, you might start or rebuild a relationship
with someone who, for reasons beyond your control, gets
on the nerves of your best friend, your parents, or someone you work with. Do you give up the relationship in
order to please these people? Or do you make it clear
that you need their support in helping your relationship,
even if they don't like the individual as you do?

As another example, what if you decide to start a new
job or you take on a new challenge in life that requires
you to spend less time and energy on someone who has
come to rely on you? Should you feel guilty? Should you
hold back from this new endeavor because it might force
you to admit your true priorities? Or do you make it
clear that you need this person's support as you take an
important step forward in your life?

These are not easy questions. Whenever you attempt
to get on with your life, you may be faced with guilt
feelings because someone else seems to be left behind. If
long ago you were taught that you must put other people's needs ahead of your own, you may feel split over
whether to take on the new challenge or hold back for
now. If it has been your habit to postpone your own

nurturance because you have been too busy nurturing someone else, you may feel conflicted whenever a situation arises in which you have to choose between charting your own path or supporting someone else's path.

"It's Time I Broke the Mold"

Paula's case illustrates this dilemma of having to choose between holding herself back or leaving someone behind. A divorced woman in her forties with one teenage daughter, Paula has wanted for several years to break off a dissatisfying relationship she'd been having with a man who needs constant attention and mothering. Yet every time Paula makes up her mind to end the relationship and get on with her life, she feels guilty because of how much this man says he needs her. In addition, she receives a host of warnings and discouragements from close friends and relatives.

For instance, Paula's best friend, Joyce, who hasn't gone out in months, thinks Paula should stay in the relationship because "the man shortage is getting worse . . . you should hold onto whatever you can find." Paula's business partner, Jordan, who tends to be very critical regardless of the subject, thinks Paula must be doing something wrong to make this man so insecure and psychosomatic. Paula's mother, Norma, who is upset that Paula hasn't remarried yet, can't understand what Paula finds so objectionable about a man who needs constant attention and mothering. She reminds Paula, "Your father, may he rest in peace, couldn't open a can of tuna fish without my help and you know we were happily married."

Certainly if Paula listened to her best friend, her business partner, or her mother, she might spend the rest of her life trying to take care of a man who refuses to take care of himself. Paula admits, "Every time we're out together, all I hear are his complaints and his excuses for why he's not making the changes he says he'd like to make. He insists he doesn't know how he'll get along without me if I leave. To tell you the truth, I have no idea how he'll get along without someone to tell him what to do. It's humorous at times, but deep down I feel responsible and I don't want to hurt him."

In order to take the next step forward in her life, Paula was going to have to work through a variety of emotional baggage. First, she was going to have to defy the studies and statistics that told her a woman her age probably will not find someone better than the man she was with. Yet that wasn't the major obstacle for Paula, as she felt, "I'm not a statistic—I'm a woman. I'm sure I'll be alone for a while, but I intend to develop a healthier relationship with someone I can respect."

The most debilitating issue for Paula, and for many women like her, was a family pattern that went back several generations. When I asked Paula to find out why she was drawn to men who were in need of mothering, she wasn't sure at first. But then when she looked into her parents' relationship and even her grandparents' marriage, a fascinating pattern began to emerge.

According to Paula, "Even though my parents often said they were happily married, in fact my mother bitterly resented that she was a strong and intelligent woman who had never been allowed to finish her education, use her talents, or do anything more than work at boring jobs to support them for a number of years until my father's business took off. From that point forward, it was my mother's job to hold herself back and do everything to keep him going. When she wanted to go out and work, he said he needed her at home too much to let her do it.

"The same thing happened with my grandmother. She

waited hand and foot on a man who was a lot less intelligent than she was. He used to make terrible business decisions because he wouldn't listen to my grandmother. Several times she had to run their store alone because he was out drinking or gambling. As far back as I can trace, it's always been strong women carrying the load for weaker men in my family."

Paula continued, "The legacy passed down to me is that I should be looking for a man just like my father and grandfather—someone who needs me so much he'll never leave me. Yet I can't respect a man like that. More importantly, I think about my teenage daughter and I know I don't want to pass this legacy of strong women taking care of weaker men down to her. I'd rather teach her that she should be looking for a relationship of equals. Yet if I can't do it for myself, how can I expect her to try?"

Even though she knew it wasn't going to be easy to let go of emotional baggage that went back several generations, Paula felt she had to make an effort. She describes how "I owe it to myself and to my daughter not to remain stuck in a dead-end relationship with someone I don't really enjoy being with. It's time I broke the mold and did what my mother and grandmother never had the opportunity to do—find a relationship where my needs are as important as the needs of the other person."

Recognizing that she was taking a huge risk, Paula nevertheless followed through on her feelings and took the next step. Within a few weeks she had broken off the relationship. She describes the feeling of being on her own again as follows: "Sure it was scary at first and I thought about giving in. After all, he was still begging me to come back and take care of him again. But then I began to enjoy being on my own and meeting a few men I really did feel good about."

For the past several months, Paula has been seeing a

divorced man who also has a teenage daughter. Will they be getting married? Paula answers, "Maybe yes and maybe not just yet. That depends on how things develop between us. But what's important is that I took the gamble and broke out of a pattern that was in my genes and was a big part of my upbringing. For that, I deserve a medal of honor."

"Walking Into a Mine Field"

Sometimes the toughest part of making a fresh start is not the struggle to leave something familiar but to enter into something that is new, unfamiliar, or threatening at first. Quite often the improvements you make in your relationships, work situation, family get-togethers, or spiritual life will be unlike anything you have experienced before. After a lifetime of knowing things to be a certain way, it may be a shock to your system to find yourself in a situation where you are being challenged to adjust to something dramatically new and different.

For example, Gwen is a thirty-four-year-old woman who spent eight years in a highly structured but not very exciting job as a layout and paste-up artist for a large graphics firm. For years she talked about quitting the firm and starting a graphics business of her own. Finally, a year ago Gwen made the big move. Then the problems began.

According to Gwen, "Being in business for myself was not what I thought it would be from reading about it in magazines and listening to upbeat 'You Can Be a Success' audiotapes. In fact, it was like walking into a mine field. Trying to land clients has been a series of painful rejections. Working on tighter deadlines has made the projects which I have obtained feel like a pressure cooker.

Dealing with late payers and people who don't keep their agreements is always a barrel of fun."

Gwen continues, "I always thought of myself as a sensitive and fragile artist. No one prepared me to be a tough businesswoman. Sometimes I come back from a meeting with a client who has been extremely critical of my work and I want to crawl in a hole and stay there. I'm not used to dealing with this many people in such high-pressure situations. When I worked for the graphics firm, it was usually just me and the materials in my cubicle. I did my job quietly, while other people had to worry about sales, cash flow, and angry customers."

When Gwen came to me for advice, she was considering going back to the kind of highly structured, large, and impersonal graphics firm she had left behind. As Gwen described, "I'm just not sure I've made the right decision. My income is still less now than it was before I started my own business. My stress levels are a whole lot higher. And there's a voice inside me that keeps saying, 'See, I knew you weren't strong enough!' "

The challenge for Gwen, and for anyone else who has taken on a major new challenge that seems overwhelming, is first to find out how to deal with the critical inner voice that says, "Quit! You can't make it. You're not strong enough. You're going to make a fool of yourself." Where does this critical inner voice come from? Why do we carry it with us into each new challenge? What can we do to make sure we don't quit too soon at something we might be able to achieve with more time and persistence?

To help Gwen deal with the problems of her start-up business, I recommended a three-step exercise you can use whenever you notice a new or difficult challenge is bringing up painful insecurities. Instead of quitting too soon or doing less than your potential, you can take the following steps:

1. Talk Back to the Critical Voice

If a part of you is saying, "Watch out! It's not going to work! You don't have what it takes!," is there yet another part of you that feels differently? Besides the frightened voice that makes you worry at night and forces you to be hesitant during the day, isn't there also a deep desire within you to take the next step, to overcome your obstacles, and to achieve your goals? If so, what could this passionate voice say to the critical/fearful voice to reduce its control over your emotions?

A technique that works extremely well for anyone who finds his or her goals and dreams are being undermined by fearful hesitations is to sit down and make a list with two columns. In the left-hand column you are to write the critical or fearful messages that have been running through your mind. Some of these might be negative things others have told you recently or long ago. In addition, the left-hand column should also include self-doubts and self-criticisms you have begun to notice yourself saying.

After you have made a substantial list of fears and criticisms in the left-hand column (at least five, no more than twenty), now comes the creative part. In the right-hand column you will be turning each negative or self-doubting message into a positive statement about yourself or what you intend to do. Make sure you select a self-affirming promise that feels accurate—don't underestimate *or* overestimate what you are capable of doing to resolve the fears listed in the left-hand column. Your job in the right-hand column will be to state clearly what you can do to refocus your efforts and renew your enthusiasm for the task that has begun to feel overwhelming.

For example, if you wrote in the left-hand column, "You never finish anything you start," then in the right-hand column you need to respond with something that is self-affirming but also true about yourself. To combat the line "You never finish anything you start," you might then put in the right-hand column, "I am getting much better at completing things now," or an even stronger response such as, "When I put my mind to something like this, it gets done no matter what obstacles arise."

The goal of this technique is to help you snap out of the defeatism and depression that can occur whenever your critical inner voice is allowed to dominate your thoughts. By talking back to your fears and self-doubts, you can restore your creative energies to do the best job possible. For example, when Gwen used this technique to combat her insecurities about running her own business, this is what she wrote:

Gwen's Critical Voice	Gwen's Passionate Voice
"You can't make it on your own. You aren't strong enough."	"I'm intelligent and persistent. If I stick with it, I'll find a way to make it succeed."
"You're too fragile to be a businesswoman. You should stick to being an artist."	"I'm not that fragile, especially when I believe in something as strongly as I believe in my ideas as an artist."
"It's not fun, and you said you wanted to do this because it would be more enjoyable."	"There are fun moments when I stop being so insecure."
"The pressure is going to do you in."	"I'm going to make sure I take real good care of myself, better care than I've ever done before."

"All this hard work is ruining your social life."

"From now on I'm going to make sure I schedule in enough time for friendships, adventures, and ways to relax. If I'm creative about it, I can make this a lot more enjoyable than it's been."

"But no one ever taught you how to be successful in business."

"I've learned tons of valuable things in the past several months. Now I just need to put my new insights and skills into practice."

Notice in Gwen's list that her critical voice seemed to want everything to be quick and immediate or else it was ready to give up. On the other hand, her passionate voice knew the deeper reasons why she had chosen to start her own business and the deeper satisfactions she was working to achieve. If you use this technique, you will find a similar phenomenon happening for yourself. Your critical voice will tell you to settle for short-cuts and underestimate your inner strength. Yet if you talk back to your fears and self-doubts, you may uncover a reservoir of passion, commitment and energy that will carry you through the hard times and help you reach your most cherished goals.

2. Remember Your Previous Moments of Courage

An extremely valuable technique to help you regain your courage and forward momentum whenever a new challenge feels overwhelming is to recall a previous time in your life when you were at the edge of quitting but you stuck to your goals and the results were satisfying.

Looking back at previous challenges in your work life, personal life, or health history, when did you feel close to giving up but, instead of quitting, you found a creative way to get through your fears and finish the task?

Even if nothing comes to mind at first, if you look deep enough into your past you will find some crucial turning point when you confronted your desire to quit and, instead, you achieved a positive outcome. It might be as seemingly minor as the time you almost cancelled a first date, a job interview, or an important meeting, yet instead of cancelling you showed up and let your best qualities shine. Or it might be as far back as a paper assignment in school, for which you stayed up all night and got the job done. It could even be a time when you almost gave up on a friendship or relationship that had become extremely difficult, but instead of going your separate ways you and this person worked out your differences and became much closer as a result. Or it could be a time when you were seriously ill or needed to start a difficult health regimen to prevent a serious illness. Even though a part of you wanted to give up and say, "There's no use," another part of you took charge and helped you regain your health.

By remembering in great detail what happened when you almost quit but instead overcame your fears, you will be giving yourself an added boost to work through whatever insecurities or external obstacles threaten to hold you back in your current challenges. For example, when Gwen used this technique to renew her energy for taking on the challenges of her start-up graphics business, she had trouble recalling a specific past triumph at first. Then she recalled an event she hadn't thought about in years.

When Gwen was a sophomore in college, she had a design class with a teacher who was extremely demanding. As Gwen recalls, "Part of me hated this teacher for being such a perfectionist, but at the same time I admired this woman for demanding so much of her students."

Near the end of the semester, Gwen had to complete a difficult design project that she had been putting off for weeks. Then the night before the assignment was due, Gwen came down with a bad case of bronchitis. Calling the teacher on the phone, she asked if she could have an extension of the deadline. The teacher said no.

Gwen describes what happened next. "I was furious. I did have bronchitis. I wasn't faking it and yet my teacher refused to budge. So I took my anger and my fears and my bronchitis into the corner of my bedroom where I spent the entire night working on this design project. Needless to say it was the best work I'd ever done in my four years of college and I've never forgotten that teacher. I think she believed in me more than I believed in myself at that time."

Even though the two experiences—completing a difficult college art project and starting in a new business as an adult—were very different, the feelings of the two challenges were similar. According to Gwen, "I can recall this tremendous urge to give up and say, 'Forget it! There's no way I'll be able to survive this challenge.' Then I dug deeper and found there was a reservoir of strength inside me I hadn't utilized before. I'm a lot more persistent sometimes than I give myself credit for."

Just as Gwen had refused to quit once before, so was it time now for her to bring up her courage and creativity again. The challenges of her new business were many and the struggle to be successful wasn't going to be resolved overnight. Yet by visualizing that she could succeed and by remembering a time in her life when she had done outstanding work by pushing herself a little harder, Gwen began to move in the right direction.

Like Gwen, each of us feels insecure and pessimistic at times. Yet if we remember how we overcame our fears and triumphed in at least one previous challenge in our lives, something clicks within our emotions. Instead of feeling helpless and weak, you can begin to feel energized and creative. Rather than focusing only on what might go wrong, you begin to develop support and good ideas for how to make things go right.

Whenever you find yourself in a new and seemingly difficult situation, take a moment and ask yourself:

> How have I managed to succeed at difficult challenges in the past? How close did I come to quitting? What happened when I didn't give up?

> What support and assistance do I need now to make this challenge less lonely and overwhelming? How can I benefit from the experience and insights of others who have been in a similar situation?

> What past examples of inner strength and persistence can I recall about myself in order to remember I have the potential to succeed in this difficult task? What inner resources can I call upon now to give me the courage to do my personal best?

Whether you know it or not, you have the power to talk yourself into taking either an important step forward or a step backward in each challenging situation you face. Unless you remember the courage and strength you carry inside, your fears and critical voices will make you believe you don't have what it takes. Only if you sit down and work through your insecurities will you be able to proceed forward to the best of your ability. Extending the Eleanor Roosevelt quote somewhat, remember that "no situation can make you feel inferior without your consent."

3. Picture Yourself Making It Happen

The final step in this three-part exercise can be the

most exhilarating and rewarding. While many people find it easy to imagine what might go wrong with a fresh start they are trying to achieve, in this technique you will have the opportunity to brainstorm how to make things go right. This can be a powerful source of good ideas and renewed self-confidence if you follow the instructions closely.

Begin by focusing on one specific fresh start that you want to make happen as a result of reading this book. What is an important step forward that you would like to make in your relationship, your work, your family situation, your spiritual search, or some other area of your life?

Be specific: What is the new beginning you would like to work on at this very moment?

Now go back and complete the first two steps, described above, for this particular challenge. First, what are the fears and self-doubts that are holding you back from this important step forward in your life? On a sheet of paper, write your hesitations and uncertainties in the left-hand column. Then turn each one of them into a positive affirmation or optimistic (but realistic) statement in the right-hand column. What can you tell yourself from your passionate voice that can reverse the pessimism of your critical voice? In the right-hand column, you should have a list of powerful statements about the persistence and creativity you have within yourself.

Next, recall a time in your life when you faced a similarly difficult or complex challenge. What did you do to overcome your insecurities and not quit when the going got rough? What support, assistance, and creative solutions did you come up with to succeed at this previous undertaking? Write down a success story from your past, or describe one to a friend or counselor. Your triumph from long ago will serve as a reminder of what you are capable of achieving if you are persistent once again.

Now comes the final step before you take action. In this crucial step you will be brainstorming several good ways to bring your idea for a new beginning into fruition. (You can use this brainstorming technique for the new beginning you mentioned above, or for any important step forward you wish to take in your life.) To help you focus on specific creative ways to increase the likelihood of your fresh start coming true, use your imagination to give honest answers to each of the following:

1. In order to make this goal happen, what self-defeating habit or self-limiting attitude from the past are you going to need to break?

2. What distraction or opposing force will you need to say no to if you are going to say yes to the new beginning you have in mind?

3. What are some of the easy things you can start doing right away to make this goal come true?

4. What are some of the more challenging or anxiety-producing things you will need to do eventually to make this important desire a reality? For each step that feels difficult or uncomfortable, come up with something you can do to get support, assistance or additional training in order to make it less stressful.

5. What is a small first step you can begin today so you can already be moving in the right direction?

6. What will be your reward if you complete this first step?

7. Who are some individuals you can call upon for support, guidance, and understanding at various stages of this endeavor?

8. What will you say to those who oppose your efforts to make progress in this area?

9. What are some of the satisfactions and joys you will experience along the way to this goal, as well as when you reach this desired outcome?

Whenever you notice you are holding yourself back from an important goal or fresh start in your life, go back to this brainstorm exercise and answer each of the above questions. You will find it frequently helps to uncover what internal or external obstacle you need to resolve. In addition, it can give you many good ideas for refocusing your energies and persisting forward.

For example, when Gwen used the above questions to regain her momentum for succeeding in her graphics business, it proved extremely helpful. According to Gwen, "I was beginning to wonder if I had enough talent or persistence to follow through with this difficult venture. Then when I looked closely at the fears that were holding me back and the people and resources I could use to overcome those fears, I knew I wasn't ready to give up just yet. With a list of specific goals, incentives, and steps in my hand, I felt a renewed sense of purpose and commitment. I'm going to make my business successful and enjoyable—I deserve it after all the hard work I've put in already."

Like Gwen, each of us has moments when we think our current challenges are too overwhelming and we feel like giving up. Yet with the tools and exercises in this book, you don't have to give up or settle for less than your potential. With the help of supportive allies and a renewed strength from within, you can keep taking small but significant steps forward.

I strongly recommend that you view this book *not* as a one-time, quickly digested essay. Instead, I urge you to refer back to it whenever you find yourself stuck in a rut or in need of creative ideas for taking the next step forward in your life. You may want to share what's contained in these chapters with friends, co-workers, and loved ones who are also in need of a fresh start, or who could benefit from letting go of some emotional baggage from the past.

Healing the hurts we carry inside is a lifelong process that takes time and persistence. Breaking through the internal and external barriers that hold us back requires patience and creativity. I applaud your efforts thus far, and I wish you lots of success as you continue to grow in your relationships, your life's work, your family, your spiritual search, and your ability to make an impact on your corner of the world. We are all survivors of that which has happened to us in the past. We are all explorers of what we can create for the future. Here's to that future!

Appendix

Suggestions for Additional Reading and Support

Some of the discussions and exercises in this book may have sparked you to resolve an important issue in your life. If so, I encourage you to keep exploring creative ways to deal with the concerns you have in mind. In this Appendix I've listed additional books and resources to help you continue making progress. If you can't find a particular book at your local bookstore or library, you can usually obtain it by: writing the publisher; calling a university library that has a larger selection; asking a bookstore, used-book dealer, or library to order it for you; or, if the book is out-of-print, you can ask your librarian or used-book dealer for a copy of the Buckley-Little Catalog, which has addresses for locating out-of-print books.

In the Introduction, I spoke briefly about several types of setbacks and losses. If you have suffered the loss of someone close to you, or any other significant hurt, you may need guidance about how to work through the stages of recovery. I recommend talking to a supportive counselor and/or reading one or more of the following books:

How to Survive the Loss of a Love, by Melba Colgrove, Harold Bloomfield, and Peter McWilliams (New York: Bantam, 1977). Written with comforting poetry and prose, as well as helpful guidelines on the stages of recovery, this book is easy to read and contains much food for thought.

When Bad Things Happen to Good People, by Harold Kushner (New York: Avon, 1983). This book is both the story of a father whose child died and the struggle of a rabbi to understand why we lose those dearest to us. It describes the importance of faith in a compassionate God who does not cause the evil around us but supports us in dealing with the struggles of our imperfect world.

Necessary Losses, by Judith Viorst (New York: Simon and Schuster, 1986). A powerful analysis of how to view life's many losses and separations in a more constructive way. The author writes with compassion and scholarly depth about the many steps each of us must take to find value and strength in the things that happen to us.

The Book of Hope: How Women Can Overcome Depression, by Helen DeRosis and Victoria Pellegrino (New York: Bantam, 1977). One of the most informative, realistic, and helpful books about dealing with mood swings and obstacles to growth.

In Chapter One, the discussion focuses on why our efforts to grow or change are often blocked by unresolved hurts from the past. If you want to unravel the obstacles in your own life, here are some additional helpful books:

Smart Cookies Don't Crumble, by Sonya Friedman (New York: Pocket, 1986). A compassionate and constructive look at what holds people back and what gives them the courage and persistence to recover from life's disappointments.

Your Inner Child of the Past, by Hugh Missildine (New York: Pocket, 1983). A classic on how to understand

and work with the unresolved feelings that go back to childhood.

Making Peace With Yourself, by Harold Bloomfield and Leonard Felder (New York: Ballantine, 1986). This book deals with the recurring phenomenon that the more we resist some part of ourselves (our Achilles' heels), the more they persist. It shows how to accept your vulnerabilities and turn them into strengths.

Adult Children of Alcoholics, by Janet Geringer Woititz (Pompano Beach, Fla.: Health Communications, 1983). If you grew up in a family with alcoholism, drug addiction, or emotional abuse, there are many ways it can affect your adult habits and relationships. This book can help you unravel why you are the way you are and what you can do to break out of old habits.

Betrayal of Innocence: Incest and Its Devastation, by Susan Forward and Craig Buck (New York: Penguin, 1978). If you were sexually molested as a child or teenager, this book can help you understand how that experience might still be affecting your life. It provides understanding and suggestions for taking the next step to undo the emotional hurt you may have kept inside.

In Chapter Two, I suggest repeatedly the importance of finding a helpful friend, counselor, or support group to assist you in working through issues from long ago. How do you find the right listener or advisor? Here are some guidelines to keep in mind:

Friends: Not all friends are good listeners. Make sure you don't choose to confide in someone who is more concerned with being right than with being a supportive listener. Set firm ground rules that you need this person's patience and understanding rather than criticism or attempts to squash your feelings. If your friend repeatedly says things like, "You shouldn't feel that way," or "You've got to stop being so sensitive," then you need to choose someone else as your listener.

Counselors: Although there are lists of psychologists, psychiatrists, and counselors in the Yellow Pages and in association directories, the most reliable way to find a qualified professional is to ask for a personal referral from a friend, relative, physician, clergy member, seminar leader, or adult education course instructor. Make sure you choose a counselor you can trust and who respects your uniqueness.

Support Groups: You can obtain a partial list of support groups by sending a self-addressed, stamped envelope to National Self-Help Clearinghouse, 33 West 42nd Street, New York, New York 10036. Be sure to specify the type of group you want. You can also call friends, relatives, doctors, clinics, and psychologists to ask about specific support groups that may exist near where you live. In addition, what works for most people is to find three to fifteen people who share a common concern and then start meeting once a week or once a month. By forming your own support group of people you can trust, you will be well on your way to resolving the issues you face.

In Chapter Three, there were specific suggestions on how to improve your relationships. For additional insights on breaking self-defeating habits, consider:

Do I Have to Give Up Me to Be Loved by You?, by Jordan and Margaret Paul (Minneapolis: Compcare, 1983). A creative and thoughtful new approach to resolving the most difficult issues in a relationship—how to combine freedom and commitment.

How to Break Your Addiction to a Person, by Howard Halpern (New York: Bantam, 1984). This book has helped many people break free of an unhealthy obsession with someone who was wrong for them.

Men Who Hate Women and the Women Who Love Them, by Susan Forward and Joan Torres (New York: Bantam, 1986). Women who have let men belittle and intimidate them need to read this book, as do men who want to learn how to create a relationship of mutual respect.

Married People: Staying Together in the Age of Divorce, by Francine Klagsbrun (New York: Bantam, 1985). An intelligent and positive look at how to revive a relationship that is stuck in roles or habits that one or both partners have outgrown.

Women Who Love Too Much, by Robin Norwood (Los Angeles: Pocket, 1986). This book explores why people stay in bad relationships, choose the wrong partners, or try to rescue a loved one who refuses to grow up.

In Chapter Four, I discuss several ways of resolving your mixed feelings about work. Here are some excellent resources to help you take the next step:

Work with Passion: How to Do What You Love for a Living, by Nancy Anderson (New York: Carroll and Graf, 1984). A very useful nuts-and-bolts approach to reexamining what you do for a living. It provides guidelines not only for choosing a career but also for overcoming the obstacles in making the switch.

What Color Is Your Parachute? by Richard Bolles (Berkeley, Calif.: Ten Speed Press, updated yearly). This is the classic in its field. It has so many different brainstorming techniques and practical bits of advice, it has become one of the best-selling books in history.

How to Manage Your Boss, by Christopher Hegarty and Philip Goldberg (New York: Ballantine, 1985). If you ever wished you could handle a difficult boss better, this book provides dozens of useful strategies. I have a special fondness for the title because when my last book was published in Italian, the listing of this title on the bibliography page had a misspelling that made it into *How to Menage Your Boss.*

How to Get Control of Your Time and Your Life, by Alan Lakein (New York: New American Library, 1974). In this handy book you will gain hundreds of good ideas about how to make your work more efficient so there is more time left over for the other priorities in your life.

Overcoming the Fear of Success, by Martha Friedman (New York: Warner, 1982). A fascinating look at why you might be holding back from achieving what you could, or why you don't feel comfortable being assertive, successful or in charge.

Go For it! by Irene Kassorla (New York: Dell, 1985). One of the most practical and realistic books written about overcoming the self-defeating habits we each possess. It focuses on why many of us were taught to be victims and how to overcome those limitations.

Enterpreneurial Mothers, by Phyllis Gillis (New York: Rawson, 1984). A down-to-earth description of what you will need to start, develop, and maintain a successful home-based business. It not only deals with marketing, finances, and networking, but also with how to balance your work with your family concerns.

In Chapter Five, several techniques for repairing a strained relationship with a difficult family member are described. In addition, you will gain insights and support from reading any of these works:

Making Peace With Your Parents, by Harold Bloomfield and Leonard Felder (New York: Ballantine, 1985). The techniques in this book can be applied as well to stepparents, in-laws, siblings, or anyone else for whom you have both love and tensions.

Once My Child, Now My Friend, by Elinor Lenz (New York: Warner, 1981). I've seen this book used by both daughters and mothers in equal numbers. It is a moving account of the struggle to break out of the ruts of mother/daughter and build something more satisfying for both individuals.

Getting to Yes, by Roger Fisher and William Ury (New York: Penguin, 1983). Primarily written to discuss win/win negotiations for business people and diplomats, it is the best approach for family conflicts, too. It describes how to let the other person feel appreciated and respected even when you disagree or have competing interests. It will give you ideas about how to settle differences with a difficult relative so that both sides feel satisfied.

Loving Someone Gay, by Don Clark (New York: New American Library, 1978). An excellent book for increasing the understanding and reducing the misinformation in families that are conflicted about gay and lesbian issues.

Beyond Acceptance: Parents of Lesbians and Gays Talk About Their Experiences, by Carolyn Welch Griffin, Marian J. Wirth and Arthur G. Wirth (Englewood Cliffs, N.J.: Prentice-Hall, 1986). A fascinating look at the stages family members go through in reacting to and rebuilding their closeness with a loved one they didn't understand at first.

No Strings Attached, by Howard Halpern (New York: Simon and Schuster, 1979). A helpful book about how family members can let go of each other long enough to discover a healthier way of reconnecting.

In Chapter Six, the discussion focused on religion, spirituality, and renewing your sense of meaning and purpose. There are numerous books on this subject, and you may want to ask people who share your religious background or beliefs for more specific recommendations. The list below is a brief sample of some of my favorite books from a variety of traditions:

Man's Search for Meaning, by Viktor Frankl (New York:

Pocket, 1959, 1985). As I described in the chapter, this book is a powerful story of how one man not only survived the concentration camps of Nazi Germany but also developed a school of therapy that focuses on our search for meaning and purpose.

Coming Home, The Experience of Enlightenment in Sacred Traditions, by Lex Hixon (Garden City, N.Y.: Anchor, 1978). An intelligent and accessible book on the inner search for spirituality that takes place in the Zen, Christian, Jewish, Sufi, Taoist, Hindu, and other traditions.

Godwrestling, by Arthur Waskow (New York: Schocken, 1978). A series of stories about an innovative Jewish study group, a *havurah,* that looks into the most challenging questions of belief, purpose, and ethics. It struggles with issues such as how to overcome the sexism and interreligious rivalries found in most religions. Copies may be difficult to find, but can be ordered for $8.95 from Schocken Books, 62 Cooper Square, New York, New York 10003.

Companions on the Inner Way, by Morton Kelsey (New York: Crossroad, 1985). Written by an ordained Christian educator who has explored various forms of meditation, journal-writing, and pastoral counseling, it offers a wealth of insights about Christianity, psychology, and the stages of spiritual insight.

Women of Spirit: Female Leadership in the Jewish and Christian Traditions, by Rosemary Ruether and Eleanor McLaughlin (New York: Simon and Schuster, 1979). A myth-shattering book on women who made an impact on Catholicism, Judaism, Evangelicals, Episcopalians, Quakers, Lutherans, Presbyterians, and several other denominations.

The Courage of Conviction, by Philip Berman (New York: Ballantine, 1986). A thought-provoking book of personal statements by well-known people on what they believe and the role spirituality plays in their lives. It shows the diversity of beliefs and practices that each of us has.

Goddesses in Everywoman, by Jean Shinoda Bolen (New York: Harper and Row, 1984). A fascinating book by a psychiatrist who looks at Greek mythology, Jungian archetypes, and the search for spirituality in a fresh way. By reading this book, you begin to recognize strengths and mysteries in yourself and others.

Finding God, by Rifat Sonsino and Daniel Syme (New York: Union of American Hebrew Congregations, 1986). Ten different ways of understanding the concept of one God are described from both a historical and a faith perspective.

The Essential Reinhold Neibuhr, by Robert McAfee Brown (New Haven: Yale, 1986). A series of essays and speeches that look deeply into Christian theology, ethics, and efforts to improve the world.

Let the Trumpets Sound: The Life of Martin Luther King, Jr., by Stephen Oates (New York: Mentor, 1985). An outstanding biography of an outstanding religious and political leader. This book can inspire you to follow through on the dream of a more just society. It describes the close connection between faith and social change.

Jewish and Female, by Susan Weidman Schneider (New York: Simon and Schuster, 1984). You haven't understood Judaism or human spirituality until you've explored the heroines, rituals, experiences, and traditions that are left out of most patriarchal sources. This is a book for women and men of varying traditions to rediscover the nonsexist potential for religion.

Cutting Through Spiritual Materialism, by Chogyam Trungpa (Boston: Shambhala Books, 1973). A challenging book by a Tibetan Buddhist spiritual leader who describes the dangers of looking for easy answers or materialistic incentives on one's spiritual path.

When All You've Ever Wanted Isn't Enough, by Harold
   Kushner (New York: Summit, 1986). Using the Book
   of Ecclesiastes and several moving current portraits,
   Rabbi Kushner describes the difficult but rewarding
   search for a life of meaning.

In Chapter Seven, there are techniques for overcoming
procrastination and fencesitting. For additional guidelines and discussions on how to make better decisions
and stick to goals, here are some excellent sources:

Procrastination: Why You Do It, What to Do About It,
   by Jane Burka and Lenora Yuen (Reading, Mass.:
   Addison-Wesley, 1983). An extremely down-to-earth
   and practical guide to understanding why you've become a staller or delayer along with several ways to
   break the pattern. The authors deal with important
   topics such as the fear of failure and the fear of success. They also provide suggestions about how to live
   and work with procrastinators.
Overcoming Indecisiveness, by Theodore Isaac Rubin (New
   York: Avon, 1986). A thorough discussion of several
   ways decisions get blocked or postponed. Using humor
   and several step-by-step techniques, the author provides realistic guidelines for breaking deadlocks and
   improving one's overall approach to making decisions.

In Chapter Eight, the discussion focuses on how to
make sure your fresh starts aren't squashed by other
people dumping their emotional baggage on you. Here
are three books that give added suggestions for dealing
with critical or difficult individuals who tend to belittle
your efforts:

Coping With Difficult People, by Robert Bramson (Garden City, N.Y.: Anchor, 1981). A helpful guide to
   several kinds of difficult people and how to deal with
   them effectively. While the book focuses on difficult

people at work, the techniques are useful in other areas of your life as well.

Nobody's Perfect, by Hendrie Weisinger and Norman Lobsenz (New York: Warner, 1983). A useful guide to understanding why people put up the resistance they do to your good ideas. It explores how to give criticism, overcome obstacles, and get results even with the most difficult individuals.

Pathfinders, by Gail Sheehy (New York: Bantam, 1982). This inspiring book shows how several well-known and not well-known individuals overcame the crises and obstacles in their lives. It describes in great detail how courage, love, and persistence are often victorious.

Index

ABOUT THE AUTHOR

LEONARD FELDER, Ph.D., is a psychologist in Santa Monica, California. His four books include MAKING PEACE WITH YOURSELF and the best-seller MAKING PEACE WITH YOUR PARENTS, which won the Book of the Year Award from *Medical Self-Care* Magazine. A regularly syndicated newspaper columnist, Dr. Felder has also written for national magazines, including REDBOOK, NEW WOMAN, SUCCESS, GLAMOUR, PARENTS, MOTHERS TODAY, SYLVIA PORTER'S PERSONAL FINANCE, WRITER'S DIGEST and PUBLISHERS WEEKLY. His books have been translated into nine languages.

Originally from Detroit, Michigan, he is a *Phi Beta Kappa* graduate of Kenyon College in Ohio, and was the Director of Research for Doubleday and Company in New York before he became a psychologist. A widely requested talk show guest and keynote speaker, Dr. Felder was presented with the Distinguished Merit Citation of the National Conference of Christians and Jews for his work to combat racism, sexism, religious prejudice, and family conflicts. For information about Dr. Felder's lectures and workshops, write to: The Publisher's Group, P.O. Box 451, Santa Monica, California 90406.